THE RENAISSANCE AND ENGLISH HUMANISM

THE ALEXANDER LECTURESHIP

THE ALEXANDER LECTURESHIP was founded in honour of Professor W. J. Alexander, who held the Chair of English at University College from 1889 to 1926. Each year the Lectureship brings to the University a distinguished scholar or critic to give a course of lectures on a subject related to English Literature.

The
Renaissance
and English
Humanism

DOUGLAS BUSH

UNIVERSITY OF TORONTO PRESS

THE ALEXANDER LECTURES

(Unless otherwise indicated the lectures have been published by the University of Toronto Press)

1929–30 L. F. CAZAMIAN: Parallelism in the recent development of English and French literature. These lectures were included in the author's *Criticism in the Making* (Macmillan, 1929)

1930–31 H. W. GARROD: *The Study of Poetry* (Clarendon, 1936)

1931–32 IRVING BABBITT: Wordsworth and modern poetry Included as "The Primitivism of Wordsworth" in the author's *On Being Creative* (Houghton, 1932)

1932–33 W. A. CRAIGIE: *The Northern Element in English Literature* (1933)

1933–34 H. J. C. GRIERSON: Sir Walter Scott Included in *Sir Walter Scott, Bart.* (Constable, 1938)

1934–35 G. G. SEDGEWICK: *Of Irony, Especially in Drama* (1934, 1948)

1935–36 E. E. STOLL: *Shakespeare's Young Lovers* (Oxford, 1937)

1936–37 F. B. SNYDER: *Robert Burns, His Personality, His Reputation, and His Art* (1936)

1937–38 D. NICHOL SMITH: *Some Observations on Eighteenth-Century Poetry* (1937)

1938–39 CARLETON W. STANLEY: *Matthew Arnold* (1938)

1939–40 J. DOUGLAS N. BUSH: *The Renaissance and English Humanism* (1939)

1940–41 No lectures given

1941–42 H. J. Davis: *Stella, a Gentlewoman of the Eighteenth Century* (Macmillan, 1942)

1942–43 H. Granville-Barker: Coriolanus
Included in the author's *Prefaces to Shakespeare: Vol. II* (Princeton, 1947)

1943–44 F. P. Wilson: *Elizabethan and Jacobean* (Clarendon, 1945)

1944–45 F. O. Matthiessen: *Henry James, the Major Phase* (Oxford, 1944)

1945–46 S. C. Chew: *The Virtues Reconciled, an Iconographical Study* (1947)

1946–47 Marjorie Hope Nicolson: *Voyages to the Moon* (Macmillan, 1948)

1947–48 G. B. Harrison: Shakespearean Tragedy
Included in the author's *Shakespeare's Tragedies* (Routledge and Kegan Paul, 1951)

1948–49 E. M. W. Tillyard: *Shakespeare's Problem Plays* (1949)

1949–50 E. K. Brown: *Rhythm in the Novel* (1950)

1950–51 Malcolm W. Wallace: *English Character and the English Literary Tradition* (1952)

1951–52 R. S. Crane: *The Languages of Criticism and the Structure of Poetry* (1953)

1952–53 No lectures given

1953–54 F. M. Salter *Mediaeval Drama in Chester* (1955)

1954–55 Alfred Harbage: *Theatre for Shakespeare* (1955)

1955–56 Leon Edel: *Literary Biography* (1957)

1956–57 James Sutherland: *On English Prose* (1957)

to

A. S. P. WOODHOUSE

Preface

THESE FOUR LECTURES deal with only a few aspects of a many-sided problem and are, of course, a very sketchy and inadequate fulfilment of their spacious title. I hope in time to treat the subject in a more substantial way. Meanwhile, though there is an unwonted joy in travelling without baggage, it is painful not to be able to record my obligations to the multitude of scholars who have written on these topics. However, the scholar will not need foot-notes and a bibliography to recognize them, and the general reader, if there is such a person, will not care. The best apology I can offer is that of the unmarried mother: "It's such a little baby."

I should like to thank the committee which administers the Alexander lectureship for its invitation, and to pay my respects to its chairman, Principal Malcolm W. Wallace, whose various studies of Tudor humanism, notably his *Life of Sir Philip Sidney*, are among the most solid contributions in that field. It is gratifying to have these discourses published by my Alma Mater, and to remember its gracious hospitality at the time of their delivery. I might add, by way of explaining some perhaps damnable iteration, that they are printed exactly as they were read.

D. B.

Cambridge, Massachusetts.

NOTE

The University of Toronto Press, in reprinting this book
for the second time, has kindly allowed me to alter some
sentences on pages 106, 108–9, and 120; the two latter
bits had long caused their author discomfort.

Contents

I.   Modern Theories of the Renaissance   13

II.   Continental Humanism   39

III.   English Humanism   69

IV.   Milton   101

    Index   135

I *Modern Theories of the Renaissance*

FOR AN ALUMNUS of the University it is an especially pleasant honour to be invited to lecture on a foundation which perpetuates the name of one of our best-loved scholars and teachers. Since my subject is classical humanism, I am glad to remember that Professor Alexander began his career as a classical scholar, and something of his characteristic sanity and clear-headedness in the criticism of modern literature may be attributed to his commerce with the ancients. It is a satisfaction to remember also, in an educational world increasingly dominated by gentiles, that the University of Toronto remains a stronghold of the humanities. And I cannot think of that without acknowledging my own debt to my instructors in the classics and English. We whose trade is lecturing loathe nothing so much as listening to other men's lectures, and I appreciate the active benevolence and fortitude which my former preceptors and friends have shown in turning out so gallantly today. Like Helen on the wall of Troy, a Helen who has at least launched a thousand foot-notes, I can look around and name the leaders of Greece. And, as Helen missed Castor and Pollux, I miss one who towered above others by his white head and broad shoulders, and whose voice when he spoke was like the snowflakes of winter.

In the first of these lectures I propose to discuss modern theories of the Renaissance; in the second and third, the character of classical humanism on the continent and in England; and in the fourth, if there should still be a quorum, the place of Milton in the humanistic tradition. Obviously this is too large a subject for even summary treatment. However, though the Renaissance is a house of many mansions, we shall not get lost if we remain standing at what I take to be the front door and simply gaze about.

Our survey of modern theories of the Renaissance may begin with a brief digression. Most of us must have encountered many times the idea that the fall of Constantinople in 1453 drove Greek scholars to western Europe and so inaugurated the great revival of the classics. In the later nineteenth and the early twentieth century this was an almost universal pedagogical doctrine, and for English-speaking readers 1453 and all that was nearly as solid as 1066. This classic myth has so long been shattered that it might be allowed to rest in pieces—or in the pages of popular writers, who so often cherish what scholars have abandoned—yet a glance at it will serve to remind us that historians are not always marching forward. While hints of the idea can be found in some early humanists, its modern formulation seems to start chiefly from Pierre Bayle and Voltaire. But the

ghost was laid in the same period in which it arose.
The first formal history of the Greek Renaissance
by an Englishman was the Latin treatise of
Humphrey Hody, posthumously published in 1742.
The very plan of this work was enough to explode
the superficial notion, for Hody's first book dealt
with Greeks in Italy during the century before
1453, the second with those who came later. Then,
in his great history of Italian literature, Tiraboschi
gave a full account of the rise of Greek in Italy in
the fourteenth and early fifteenth centuries. Gibbon cited and followed both Hody and Tiraboschi.
Hallam took a similar path in his *Introduction to
the Literature of Europe* (1837-9). How, we may
ask, did a broad historical perspective shrink into
a tight little formula? For the English-speaking
world one suspects the prime agency of such
popular books as Seebohm's *Oxford Reformers*
(1867) and the *Short History* (1874) of J. R. Green.
Of course modern scholars would not minimize the
effect of Turkish pressure on the East, but they
would not exaggerate it either, and certainly would
not tie it to a date.

From this foot-note on a particular and obsolete
error we may turn to confront error in more
complex and subtle forms. In other words, we turn
to consider modern views of the Renaissance. We
realize at once that we are concerned, not with
the mere revival of classical culture or the fine

arts, but with the whole civilization of Europe
during three or four centuries. The greatly
enlarged content of the word has enlarged the
scope of historical interpretation and multiplied
the possibilities of misinterpretation. The historian
of literature finds himself jostled by historians of
art, philosophy, religion, science, economics, and
sociology. Every group stresses a set of ideas from
which other groups derive, if not poison, at any
rate inadequate nourishment. Indeed the quest of
a satisfying formula for the Renaissance is doomed
from the start. Imagine some historian of 2500
A.D. trying to define, say, the civilization of the
United States in the early twentieth century in the
light of its literature. He will see that it was an
age of realistic revolt, and he will summon such a
cloud of witnesses—assuming for the moment that
they are all then extant—as Theodore Dreiser,
H. L. Mencken, Sinclair Lewis, Edgar Lee Masters,
Eugene O'Neill, John Dos Passos, Ernest Heming-
way, Robinson Jeffers, William Faulkner, Erskine
Caldwell, and James T. Farrell. The obvious
verdict will be that the United States was popu-
lated by commercial brigands, Fundamentalists,
blind reactionaries, drunkards, wastrels, hypo-
crites, fools, knaves, gunmen, and perverts, that
no ray of intelligence, culture, virtue, or idealism
could pierce the darkness. Our historian might pos-
sibly find some support for this view in contem-

porary Canadian newspapers. But suppose another historian with another set of preconceptions surveys the same period. The typical American voice of Vachel Lindsay assures him that the American soul was in tune with the Y.M.C.A. Robert Frost shows the homely goodwill and integrity of rural life. Willa Cather celebrates pioneer courage and traditional religious faith. The South of Ellen Glasgow is the home, not of degraded bestiality, but of highly civilized conversation and behaviour. Such philosophic moralists as Irving Babbitt and Paul Elmer More make a stern appeal to order and authority. And so on. Yet these completely different pictures can be made out of the literature of one country over one short period. What of the civilization of half a dozen countries over several hundred years?

The fallacy of attempting to compress bewildering diversity into a neat definition may seem too obvious a point to be laboured, yet this very fallacy is found not merely in popular books but in the learned theories of the Renaissance we are about to survey. It is the special privilege of the journalistic mind, which is not limited to journalists, to juggle airily with such large phrases as "the spirit of antiquity," "the spirit of the Middle Ages," "the spirit of the Renaissance," but scholarship also, in the enormous controversial literature of the last sixty years, would provide

Bacon with a new set of illustrations for his idols of the tribe, cave, market-place, and theatre. Every scholar is admirably acute in exposing the weakness of others' interpretations, and then he produces one of his own no less vulnerable than the rest. This may sound as if I were prepared to conclude by flourishing the only real master-key. I wish I were, but I cannot promise more than fulfilment of that old definition of a scholar—a siren which calls attention to a fog without doing anything to dispel it.

The traditional modern definition of the Renaissance, the definition which is still generally prevalent, may be said to start from Michelet's *History of France in the Sixteenth Century* (1855). ∨The fervent Michelet saw history not as a heap of stones but as the record of the soul and original thought, of fruitful enterprise, heroic action, heroic creation. These qualities the Renaissance displayed on every level of human culture and achievement. The bizarre, monstrous, and prodigiously artificial Middle Ages broke down with the discovery of the world and the discovery of man. This last phrase in particular was to echo through generations of historians.

Five years later, in 1860, appeared Burckhardt's *Civilization of the Renaissance in Italy*. Under Michelet's inspiration Burckhardt painted his brilliant picture of the Italian Renaissance as a

distinct cultural phenomenon born of the marriage
of Italian genius with the civic freedom of Italian
cities, and characterized by untrammelled individualism, by the free play of personality in life,
thought, art, and letters.   This individualism
meant a revolt against the bondage and the uni-
form solidarity of the medieval religious, moral,
and social order, the assertion of critical reason
against authority, of the senses against asceticism,
of the claims of earth against those of heaven. To
the classical revival Burckhardt assigned a large
but secondary importance. Men emancipated from
the fantastic bonds of the Middle Ages found the
dry light of antiquity a helpful guide to the understanding of the physical and intellectual world,
and often, under a rosier light, they worshipped
Bacchus and Venus with new ardour.

If Burckhardt in his broad view of Italian
civilization perhaps underestimated the significance of the classical tradition, a notable supplement had already appeared in 1859, that work of
Georg Voigt which in its revised form is still useful.
Some of Voigt's leading ideas anticipated Burckhardt. He saw Italy as the creator of Renaissance
culture, the one bridge between the ancient and
the Christian world. The classics encouraged the
individualism which the medieval church had
suppressed and, in spite of religious motives in a
number of men, the movement tended toward

literary, frivolous, and immoral neo-paganism. However, since Voigt has had a much more specialized influence than Burckhardt, we may stick to the latter.

Burckhardt's picture of the Renaissance, drawn with an artist's hand, makes a relatively simple and coherent pattern and for generations it has been commonly accepted as one of the established absolutes of history. For the historically minded, however, history contains no absolutes. We can never sit down with the sense of possessing the past or any part of it. All that we do possess is our own particular view, which changes from age to age not only with fuller inquiry but with the changing conditions of the observer. It would be absurd to deny that chapter and verse can be abundantly quoted in support of all the essential terms of Burckhardt's definition. But it must also be said that every one of those terms has been seriously questioned or flatly rejected by many modern scholars. At the same time it is a testimony to the power of Burckhardt's synthesis that all subsequent theories can be most conveniently discussed in relation to his, and his theory still has its defenders. Our survey of the problem is necessarily limited to a few main ideas, and there is small room for the qualifications which are needed at every turn.

First there is the theory that Italy was the

precocious and prolific mother of the Renaissance and that the rest of Europe received its stimulus from her. On the classical side especially that view has been traditional since the time of the early Italian humanists, who regarded themselves as the direct heirs of ancient Rome and as the teachers of the barbarous nations beyond the Alps. However, taking the Renaissance in its conventional broad meaning, we may say that some critics of Burckhardt have agreed that the movement was Italian but have completely disagreed about its essential character, and other critics have minimized or rejected the argument for Italian origins. Within these two groups, moreover, there have been wide differences of opinion.

For Burckhardt the Italian Renaissance embodied a rationalistic and naturalistic revolt of the individual against Christian faith and Christian ethics—a theory which readily lent itself to Nietzschean heightening. But some of Burckhardt's earlier and later critics have urged that Italian individualism, far from being anti-Christian, was very positively Christian, and found its most germinal expression in the mysticism of Joachim of Flora and St. Francis of Assisi. That undogmatic and subjective faith, with the new and intimate love for the natural world felt by St. Francis, rejuvenated Italian Catholicism and inspired Italian art. This general impulse, by the way, had been touched by such writers as Michelet and Pater, though they stopped short of modern theories. The doctrine of Franciscan mysticism has had eloquent champions but, like other arguments for single sources and motives, it raises at least as many questions as it settles. We do not need to think of Italian culture of the later period as neo-pagan to have difficulty in regarding as its tutelary genius the St. Francis who was not an individualist outside the church and was not sympathetic toward literature and art. Yet the spiritual influence of St. Francis was great and his ascetic ideal passed, in union with the Stoic ideal of *paupertas*, into early Italian humanism.

In its original form this theory may be called the first serious challenge offered to Burckhardt. Its chief value—or, as some would say, its romantic fallacy—has been its assertion of the place of religion in a movement traditionally regarded as almost wholly secular and irreligious. From that general position various scholars have advanced in various directions. Konrad Burdach has seen not so much a Renaissance of art or of classical culture but rather an ideal and a process of re-generation. He traces, from ancient times down, the persistent dream of a golden age, of a renewed youth and perfection. In the course of the fourteen hundred years after Christ this dream is nourished and broadened by several impulses, by man's

instinctive hope of a better day to come, by the
Christian conception of spiritual rebirth, by the
Franciscan linking of such individual regeneration
with the regeneration of the church, and finally,
in Dante, Petrarch, and others, by the vision of
a regenerated and united Italy under an emperor
who is both Caesar and Messiah. Of this comprehensive and half-mystical ideal the concrete symbol
is the eternal city. Hence an episode that historians
have dismissed as a fiasco Burdach sees as a great
moment, the spectacular attempt of Petrarch's
friend, Cola di Rienzo, to re-establish the Roman
state.

This theory, though impressively set forth,
illustrates again the fallacy of trying to open all
doors with one key, or rather of shutting one's
eyes to all doors except that for which one has the
key. In making the word "Renaissance" contain
the meanings he gives it, Burdach has to strain a
great deal out of the evidence; the weak links in
his chain of argument are strengthened by imaginative reconstruction. Further, while the theory
helps to illuminate the age of Dante and Petrarch,
Burdach does not succeed in showing that the
ideal he describes had a real effect on the age of
the Renaissance proper. Indeed, since he finds
the ideal of regeneration active through a vast
tract of time, he might have put "the Renaissance"
in ancient Egypt or Rome. Of the theory as a

whole one may say again that the solid residue is the author's cogent insistence on the religious character of Renaissance humanism.

A more recent religious interpretation of the Renaissance is that of Giuseppe Toffanin. For him individualism, in Burckhardt's sense of the word, is a late medieval phenomenon and a short-lived one. Toffanin sees classical humanism rising, not as a contributory cause of irreligious individualism, but as an anti-individualistic wall of learned orthodoxy. The spirit of the age of transition from medievalism to modernity is a faith in the progressive and final religious and cultural unity of the world under the auspices of classical humanism. Humanism has a bond of union with scholasticism, for both originated in an anti-democratic and anti-heretical impulse. Like scholasticism, humanism arrested for a time the eruption of the various rationalistic and naturalistic forces which we call modern. In concentrating on the Italian humanistic tradition, which many writers of late have tended to neglect or disparage, Toffanin may perhaps be charged, like other theorists, with a too narrow exclusiveness, yet to me at least the tradition of Christian humanism seems a broad and central road. Toffanin's view of a strong Italian orthodoxy is, I think, fundamentally sound, and one large result is the emergence of the true harmony, rather than the conventional differences, between Italian and northern humanism. But this subject must be postponed for the present.

We may turn now to those theories which reject the notion of Italy as the matrix of the Renaissance. The only other country which can be set up as a rival is France—that is, pending an official proclamation from Germany of purely Teutonic origins. The significance of medieval French culture was already a commonplace in the time of Pater's volume, and some modern scholars have urged that the Renaissance was not Italian and of the fifteenth century, but French and of the twelfth. All the manifestations of ripe culture found in Italy, from conversation to cathedrals, are found in France at an earlier date—civilized towns and polished courts; cultivated society in which women play an important role; an abundant and sophisticated literature; achievements in the fine and useful arts; and so on. In many things, such as the romances of chivalry and the lyrical poetry of love, France is the teacher of Italy. Even the classical primacy of the Italians may be questioned. Old French literature shows wide and intelligent knowledge and adaptation of the Latin classics. The classical revival under Charlemagne, which caused Bishop Modoin to exclaim that golden Rome was reborn for the world, was carried on in such centres as Chartres and flowered in the great renaissance of the twelfth century. This early renaissance was of major importance on the classical side and it was still more important in the development of philosophy, science, and mathematics. And all this fertile activity is going on in France before Italy is well awake. As even a summary partly indicates, this thesis can be carried to extreme lengths, as it has been by Johan Nordström, and we find a French scholar declaring, for instance, that until the sixteenth century English literature was hardly more than an off-shoot of French! But even chauvinistic claims may have an ultimately salutary effect. We cannot ignore the international character of medieval culture and isolate the French or the Italian Renaissance as a purely self-contained phenomenon.

The various strands of our large problem are too closely interwoven to be kept separate and the question of Italian origins has already partly anticipated the question of chronology. We must have some rough chronological limits in mind when we use the word "Renaissance." Even if we use it to indicate an individual outlook and attitude we imply that there was some period when that outlook and attitude were characteristic and dominant, or as characteristic and dominant as a particular *Weltanschauung* ever is in any age. Burckhardt saw the Renaissance as beginning in Italy in the fourteenth century and reaching its

climax around 1500. It was a simple matter for
him, since Renaissance day banished medieval
night, and the few gleams of individualism that he
discerned in the Middle Ages, such as the Goliardic
songs, were obviously the first rays of dawn.
Michelet had already taken a wider view. He had
in fact observed so many medieval expressions of
individualism that he was compelled to ask why
the Renaissance arrived three hundred years later
than it should have. The answer seemed to be
that the medieval mind, entrenched behind its
walls of religious conservatism and superstition,
stubbornly resisted the forces making for a return
to nature. Of later nineteenth-century historians,
some saw the Middle Ages as a broad plain,
without much on it but churches and monasteries,
sloping up slightly from the early barbarian period
and then rising suddenly to a mountain range.
For others the plain was studded with hills, but
they were the foothills of the Renaissance. When
we stop to think of it, the term "Middle Ages,"
though both the phrase and the idea have a long
pedigree, is unhistorical. It implies that a period
of a thousand years, a fairly large segment in the
recorded life of man, was not itself, an integral
and consecutive part of the great panorama, but
a sort of interlude between the two periods which
really mattered.   André Maurois somewhere
caricatures the unhistorical attitude by having a

knight address his followers in this fashion: "In truth, then, we men of the Middle Ages must not forget that to-morrow we set off for the Hundred Years' War."

One reason for the general readiness to play fast and loose with the Middle Ages has been the general ignorance which has prevailed until a relatively recent time. William Morris was a medieval enthusiast, with great knowledge in some directions, yet his conception of the medieval world was quite unrealistic. Of late years we have had the religious, social, and alcoholic romanticism of Chesterton and Belloc, the twin exponents of "the Mass and Maypole" school of history. And many secularly minded people still believe that the Middle Ages were romantic, though a medieval knight, sitting down at a modern breakfast-table beside a toaster and a percolator, would think he had been transported out of his own prosaic world into the land of Prester John. But the more serious fault of serious historians has been the drawing of picturesque contrasts between the religiosity of the Middle Ages and the paganism of the Renaissance. Symonds, for example, can indulge in a paragraph like this, in which you will observe, incidentally, the usual echoes of Michelet:

During the Middle Ages man had lived enveloped in a cowl. He had not seen the beauty of the world, or had seen it only to cross himself, and turn aside and tell his beads and pray; . . . humanity had passed, a careful pilgrim, intent on the terrors of sin, death, and judgment, along the highways of the world, and had scarcely known that they were sightworthy or that life is a blessing. Beauty is a snare, pleasure a sin, the world a fleeting show, man fallen and lost, death the only certainty, judgment inevitable, hell everlasting, heaven hard to win; ignorance is acceptable to God as a proof of faith and submission; abstinence and mortification are the only safe rules of life: these were the fixed ideas of the ascetic mediaeval Church. The Renaissance shattered and destroyed them, rending the thick veil which they had drawn between the mind of man and the outer world, and flashing the light of reality upon the darkened places of his own nature. For the mystic teaching of the Church was substituted culture in the classical humanities; a new ideal was established, whereby man strove to make himself the monarch of the globe on which it is his privilege as well as destiny to live. The Renaissance was the liberation of the reason from a dungeon, the double discovery of the outer and the inner world.

At least we should acknowledge that Jean de Meung and Chaucer wore their cowls with a difference, even if they did not enjoy life like Savonarola and Calvin.

To return to the specific problem of chronology, modern critics may be roughly divided into two camps. One view extends the Renaissance backward to include the Middle Ages, the other extends the Middle Ages forward to include the Renaissance. It may serve as a useful warning of my own set of prejudices if I say that I incline to the latter.

These two groups often appear in unnecessarily rigid opposition, when logic as well as history would recommend a compromise, but they have one basic attitude in common; they do insist on an historical continuity which makes the Middle Ages and the Renaissance much more alike than they used to be thought. The great watershed of the Renaissance has been, if not levelled down, at any rate made a less conspicuous eminence than it was. If we take the metaphysical view of man and the universe to be the most fundamental criterion, some scholars would say that the later Middle Ages and the seventeenth century witnessed more essential and far-reaching changes than the intervening period. The wholesale introduction of Aristotle in the twelfth century enabled St. Thomas Aquinas to build his great structure of rational theology; it also started the stream of scientific rationalism which was to undermine that structure; and these two movements, especially the latter, may be said to have given the modern mind its direction. At the same time, to be indecisively and exasperatingly judicial, undue insistence on continuity and undue depreciation of the Renaissance may result in missing the woods for the trees, in blurring really significant alterations in the contours of the spiritual landscape. That has been a danger in modern scholarship, a danger which is perhaps being illustrated in these discourses, but our concern at the moment is with the older attitude which brought on the reaction just described.

Depreciation of the Middle Ages has had a number of more or less traditional reasons behind it. One has been noticed, the lack of real knowledge and understanding of medieval culture. Another reason is that historians have been over-ready to take at its face value the scorn which many Renaissance humanists and neoclassicists felt for things medieval, such as degenerate scholasticism and Gothic art. A future historian would be injudicious if he allowed his estimate of the Victorian age to be guided by twentieth-century rebels against effete Victorianism. Thirdly, there has come down from the sixteenth and seventeenth centuries a considerable Protestant prejudice against the Catholic Middle Ages. Finally, and perhaps chiefly, the Michelet-Burckhardt conception of the Renaissance, which has been so congenial to the modern mind, while it was, to be sure, based on historical research, was also largely predetermined by the philosophic outlook of its authors. It was, in short, a conception engendered by modern secular liberalism, by the nineteenth-century faith in rationalistic enlightenment and progress. From that point of view the Middle Ages appeared as not much more than a long cultural lag, a period in which man was enslaved by a system based on religious super-

stition and unnatural restraint. Hence anything
in the way of revolt was a step toward the Renaissance and, ultimately, toward the triumphant
freedom of the nineteenth century.

As I have remarked already, Burckhardt's
conception of the Renaissance is still the popular
one, and there are still scholars who celebrate the
secularizing of the human mind, its emancipation
from the shackles of superstition. But nowadays
such verdicts command less immediate assent than
they once did. As we look around our world and
consider where the emancipated mind has landed
us, we may think that liberal historians might be
a little less complacent about progress. And, in
spite of our long subservience to secular liberalism,
the climate of opinion in some quarters has
changed a good deal. Voices can be heard declaring
that the Renaissance, so far as it involved a secular
revolt, was more of a calamity than a triumph.
Our concern, however, is with less nostalgic and
more historical ideas. On the one hand we might
defend the Middle Ages by saying that they were
full of rebels against religious, ethical, social, and
political authority. But such a defence, though
obvious and true, is not the one I would choose
to offer. The Middle Ages can rest sufficient claims
to greatness on their leaders of orthodoxy, however
important the rebels may have been. On the other
hand, until quite recent times historians, partly

through prejudice and partly through ignorance, have much exaggerated the suddenness and completeness of the Renaissance emancipation from medievalism. Since these lectures will be largely occupied with some Good Things which the Renaissance inherited from the Middle Ages, we can afford to admit that many Bad Things also survived. The so-called enlightenment did not banish astrology and witchcraft; indeed such sciences flourished with fresh vigour. And countless other irrational and uncritical beliefs and habits of mind persisted not merely among the multitude but among the educated, including such heralds of modernity as Bodin and Bacon and Descartes.

It is self-evident that the Renaissance, even in its narrower meaning of a classical revival, was a heterogeneous movement which contained many mutually antagonistic impulses. Without forgetting the various pitfalls of generalization we have encountered, and without denying the importance, the necessity, of the rebellious side of the Renaissance, I wish in these discussions to emphasize the more neglected and, I think, more truly representative elements of orthodox conservatism. That means, of course, emphasis on the continued strength of medieval attitudes and ways of thought, in union with a richer and fuller appreciation of the classics than medieval men ordinarily possessed.

3

To put the matter briefly and somewhat too bluntly, in the Renaissance the ancient pagan tradition (which does not mean neo-paganism), with all its added power, did not overthrow the medieval Christian tradition; it was rather, in the same way if not quite to the same degree as in the Middle Ages, absorbed by the Christian tradition. And that, after all, is only what we would, or should, expect.

If we are more accustomed to think of the Renaissance in terms of emancipation and rebellion and are more familiar with the rebels than with the conservatives, it is partly because all the world loves a rebel and partly, as I have said, because the historians have stressed what appealed to them. We look at the voluptuous Venuses of the Italian painters and exclaim, "How typical of the Renaissance lust of the eye and pride of life!" But why are they more typical than the multitudinous Madonnas of the same period? For one person who has heard of Vittorino da Feltre, the Christian humanist whose teaching flowered in the culture of Urbino, a score have heard of that really insignificant scoundrel, Pietro Aretino. It is a *cliché* of English literary history that Marlowe is the very incarnation of the pagan Renaissance. But is Marlowe's half-boyish revolt against traditional faith and morality more, or less, typical and important than Hooker's majestic exposition of the workings of divine reason in divine and human law?

Before we leave general definitions of the Renaissance for classical humanism, I should like to dwell a bit longer on the theory of individualism. There is not much time for it, but one may ask a few questions. In the first place, was the medieval church so crushing a weight upon the individual? One might reply that Chaucer's pilgrims do not seem to feel crushed. On a more philosophic if not necessarily a more convincing level one might appeal to the thoroughgoing moral individualism of Aquinas. It is dubious history as well as dubious praise to claim for the Renaissance the distinction of having established immoral individualism. If that were true, the medieval church would have had an easier task than it had.

But, it may be said, was not Protestantism itself the expression of Renaissance individualism *par excellence?* While on the one hand Protestantism made every man his own priest, on the other it substituted the absolute authority of the Bible for the authority of the church. And if in practice the medieval church was often repressive, it was less so than Protestantism, as soon as the latter achieved organization and power. Besides, we must remember that the Reformation was only the climax of a widespread medieval movement;

Luther's chief guides, apart from the Bible, were Augustine and medieval pietists.

In the field of political thought there is the bogeyman of Europe, the exponent of unscrupulous Italian individualism. Machiavelli was a conscientious official and ardent patriot who was daring enough to find lessons for his troubled time and country in the pages of Livy. His ideal was not the despotism of the ruthless strong man, it was the ancient Roman republic; but he believed that despotism might be a necessary prelude to a republic, since only the strong man could create order out of chaos. Machiavelli's view of the state, as his avowed modern disciple has realized, has much in common with Fascism. Further, his supposedly revolutionary doctrine of expediency was in the main a formulation of the principles on which medieval statecraft had operated. As Professor J. W. Allen remarks, in connection with Machiavelli, the further you go into the political thought of the sixteenth century, the more medieval you will find it.

In the field of personal ethics there is that philosophic individualist, Montaigne, who devotes his life to the study of himself as he is, without excuses and without unduly exacting aspirations, and who seems to be, in his quiet ironic way, a solvent of all traditional external restraints. Yet, although Montaigne draws his rationalism from the classics and from himself, he respects religion as a plane of experience above his own. And he is a good if not over-active Catholic, partly by instinct and inheritance, but much more because he believes in the necessity and efficacy of the church as a bulwark of solidarity. Moreover, if Montaigne secularizes personal ethics, he is no modern advocate of "self-expression." He had a large share in creating the ideal of the *honnête homme*, and the very definition of the civilized man is that he obeys standards of good taste, a norm of rational behaviour free from individual eccentricities. Thus, however much Montaigne might be invoked by *libertins*, he is to be found on the side of order, authority, reason. His essays may be called, in the words of Lanson (who makes due qualifications), the great reservoir from which is to flow the classic spirit.

But this catalogue of queries—they are not rounded judgments—might be prolonged forever, and we may end with a glance at the great mass of miscellaneous literature of the age of individualism. And what are the literary rebels doing all over Europe? Trying to write like the ancients. From the Ciceronians who aped their master in his own tongue to the men who strove to endow vernacular prose with the ease and power of Latin, from the lyrists who toiled to bury medieval genres under the dignified weight of odes, hymns, and pastorals, to the heroic poets like Ariosto and Spenser who consciously raised medieval romance to the epic plane—everywhere, and not merely among rigorous classicists, we find the same motives and ideals. It was this age of individualism which gave the venerable doctrine of imitation more devout endorsement than it ever had before or has had since; which enthroned Aristotle and Horace as arbiters of poetic theory and practice and created a code of dogmatic rules for the drama; which professed and largely worked in the classical and medieval faith that the purpose of literature is delightful teaching.

Altogether, our theory of the Renaissance must be, like the Copernican hypothesis, the simplest theory which explains the phenomena. That of rebellious individualism is much too simple and exclusive.

II *Continental Humanism*

SOME SURVEY OF THEORIES of the Renaissance as a whole has been a necessary prelude to concentration on one special phase of it, classical humanism. The complex literary and philosophic tendencies of the Renaissance can be best understood if we regard the humanistic tradition as the central road and other more or less antagonistic movements as departures from that road. With all its changing aspects humanism, in the twelfth century or the fourteenth or the sixteenth, is an essentially homogeneous thing, and before approaching it more closely we might for a moment rise above the clouds of definitions and particulars to view the classical Renaissance from a height which obliterates all but the major contours. We see then that, just as young, crude, and virile Rome was educated by conquered Greece, so in time captive Rome took captive her conquerors, the young, crude, and virile barbarians of western Europe. If we knew no history at all after 476, to take a nominal date, we could not fail to predict the general development of the next thousand years. It is a repetition, in new conditions and with new results, of the same inevitable cultural process. What re-emerges now is Graeco-Roman culture, at first in a few small and scattered oases which had deep roots; then, though some oases

wither, most of them enlarge and multiply until
Europe is once more a civilized continent. The
recovery of antiquity, from being a dim ideal,
becomes an accomplished fact. Yet this Graeco-
Roman culture is something new, for it has been
modified by the northern culture in which it has
risen. Above all it has been fundamentally changed
by Christianity. These generalizations are equally
spacious and elementary, but it is well to have a
large perspective in mind, since it reduces national
and temporal factors to a properly subordinate
place. Classical humanism must always be considered in European terms.

From the Middle Ages onward humanists may
be divided according as their preoccupations are
literary or philosophic. On the one side we have
enthusiastic collectors of books, elegant stylists,
studious readers, and, as learning becomes critical,
"pure scholars" in the modern sense of the phrase.
Of these some were sincere devotees of Christianity
and some preferred not to bring it into private
life. Without disparaging such men's services to
learning, we may neglect them here for the
philosophic humanists who regarded the classics
as a means rather than an end, who sought to
apply classical wisdom to the uses of education
and life, and who, in short, created humanism as
a cultural ideal and discipline. Of course we
cannot draw a rigid line between these categories,

since many men have a foot on each side of the fence, yet there is seldom any doubt, if the metaphor will stand the strain, which side their hearts are on. It is not begging the question to base our definition of humanism on the men of ideas rather than on the men of words and books. Intellectually and spiritually the former were much more important, and numerically they made an impressive phalanx. It might be begging the question to use the terms "philosophic humanists" and "Christian humanists" interchangeably, but it is permissible and essential to examine the relations between classical culture and Christianity and interrogate as many as we can of the men generally taken as representatives of the humanistic tradition.

The acceptance of pagan literature by the Christian world was naturally not achieved without a struggle. Art is suspect to some kinds of puritans in all times and places. Indeed it might be said, with due reservations, that Plato and William Prynne are brothers under the skin. Imaginative literature is a pale and distorted imitation of truth; it is sometimes irreligious and immoral; and it stirs up emotions which should be restrained. To Platonic grounds of hostility the devout Christian added others. At the best classical literature was pagan and earth-bound, and distracted the soul from its heavenward pilgrimage. At the worst, its sceptical rationalism sapped religious faith and its sympathetic or sensual treatment of love sapped morality. Such charges have been made in every century from Plato's to our own and, if the Fathers' antagonism was sometimes violent, in the circumstances it could hardly be otherwise; and we must remember that some of them loved the classics. We must remember too that classical literature was never more often attacked than it was throughout the centuries of Renaissance enlightenment.

Early in the Christian era practical necessities brought about a rational compromise. The language of the church and of religious literature had to be learned and it could be learned only by study of its great masters. Besides, Christians could not defend their faith against pagans if they had not mastered their opponents' weapons, both rhetorical and philosophical. In addition to such utilitarian reasons it could be urged that much pagan literature was positively edifying, even for earnest Christians. For example, the Bible provided no detailed system of everyday ethics and since, in the intervals of exercising faith, hope, and charity, men might have occasion for justice, prudence, temperance, and fortitude, the moral works of Cicero and Seneca made an invaluable supplement to the inspired writings. Even pagan poetry might be elevating, such as the Virgil every schoolboy studied, and holy Chrysostom, as Mil-

ton says, had the art to cleanse the scurrilous
vehemence of Aristophanes into the style of a
rousing sermon. Thus the claims of pagan literature, among which one need not omit aesthetic
appeal, had to be acknowledged. In spite of
periodical attacks the position of classical authors
in the Christian world became more and more
secure. Before talking about patristic or medieval
illiberality we should not forget that at least up
to the sixteenth century education and culture
were largely promoted and maintained by ecclesiastical effort; that throughout that period, and far
beyond it, ecclesiastical authority gave pagan
writings a place in education which the modern
liberal would never dream of giving to religious
works; and that it was mainly churchmen who
copied and preserved the ancient authors for often
ungrateful men of the Renaissance to "discover."

If pagan literature thus entered the Christian
world through the front door, it also got in, partly
disguised, through the back door of allegorical
interpretation. Yet one should not say "back
door," since allegorical interpretation is almost as
old as literature itself. It was fully developed
before Plato. Greek thinkers sought support for
their several doctrines in the old myths, and the
theory that the myths embodied hidden truth
could also be invoked by rationalists or pietists
who wished to defend Homer and Hesiod from

charges of impiety in their tales of the gods. We cannot pause over the various methods of exegesis, scientific, euhemeristic, and moral, nor can we follow the later adaptation of allegory to the Old and the New Testament. Here too it could be used for different purposes, to prove that the Bible contained Greek philosophy, to elucidate even simple stories on the general assumption of a deeper truth, or to explain away incredible or offensive items. We can appreciate the power of the method if we recall Augustine's gratitude to Ambrose for his allegorical explanation of religious fables "which when I understood literally, I was slain." It was inevitable that the same magical sword and buckler should be grasped by apologists for the classics. The great example, of course, is Fulgentius' interpretation of the *Aeneid* as the moral life of Everyman, a pilgrim's progress. The modern lover of Virgil will smile at the deadly literalness of application—though Fulgentius is no worse than some modern topical critics of Shakespeare—yet he will hardly dare to affirm that the main idea was altogether absent from the poet's mind.

It is dangerous to broach so large and fascinating a subject as the allegorical tradition, and I will only emphasize three things. First, the allegorical method, with all its apparently wild system of correspondences on different planes, grows out of the deepest conviction of the medieval mind, the conviction of the unity of God and man, of all things in heaven and earth. Secondly, allegorical interpretation did not begin or end in the Middle Ages. To name only two late exemplars, Bacon, the modern man, gave one whole book and countless bits in other books to the scientific, moral, and political allegorizing of myths, and one of the largest works of the kind in English, George Sandys' commentary on Ovid, appeared in 1632. Thirdly, while the flame of allegory was almost extinguished by the rationalism of the later seventeenth century, it never quite went out, but burned up again in the life-giving air of romanticism. For, as Keats's debt to Sandys reminds us, a mode of conceiving myth which we may think of as naïve wrongheadedness can rise into the richest poetic metaphor and symbolism.

Mr. Spingarn begins his standard book with the statement that "the first problem of Renaissance criticism was the justification of imaginative literature." Such a view is coloured by that secular liberalism to which I have referred; it implies that the didactic conception of literature was the dead hand of medievalism. But the notion of art as self-expression and of criticism as aesthetic disinterestedness is quite modern, and it reached the logical end of its relatively short life in the gospel and practice of art for art's sake. To

see how dead that doctrine is one has only to look
at the significant poetry of the last twenty-five
years. Aestheticism has been merely an occasional
ripple on the surface of the broad deep stream of
the didactic faith which has flowed from the
beginning of literature to the present. Plato has
been mentioned. Aristotle, though comparatively
detached and objective, has ethical values con-
tinually in mind. But since we cannot run
through Greek writers down to Plutarch, it is
enough to recall one who might be thought a
dubious witness: no medieval author believes more
sincerely than Aristophanes that it is the function
of the poet to make good citizens. For the still
more practical Romans one may cite Horace, who
supplied the Renaissance with so many of its
critical precepts, especially the mixture of *utile*
and *dulce*. And one cannot pass by those deities
of the Renaissance, Cicero and Quintilian, who
said that the good orator—for posterity that meant
the poet as well—must first of all be a good man.
It was left for a much more advanced age to show
that he must be a bad one. In a word, most Greek
and Roman literature rests on the belief that a
serious author is a moral teacher. In the Middle
Ages that belief was, of course, greatly fortified by
Christianity, and if it was sometimes held with
painful literalness, as it often has been since, it
was also held by Dante. The Renaissance in-

herited the Christianized didactic tradition of the
Middle Ages and gave it an added strength
derived from fuller knowledge, admiration, and
understanding of the ancients. If the task of the
Renaissance was the justification of imaginative
literature as divorced from its moral and social
function, then it obviously failed, for it would not
be easy to name many important poets or critics
who did not preach and practise the venerable and
universal faith. After all, is not that faith the
natural and inevitable basis of most of the greatest
writing of all ages?

These general remarks will become concrete if
we consider the attitude toward literature, life,
and religion expressed by some typical humanists.
We can begin with no better representative than
that sturdy flower of twelfth-century culture, John
of Salisbury, a man who comes into the historical
spotlight at one dramatic moment, the murder of
Thomas Becket. John was the first medieval man
to write with full knowledge of Aristotle's *Organon*.
He was master of all the large body of Latin
literature extant in his time, and he defended it
gladly against its enemies. Virgil he sees as the
world-philosopher who, in the form of fable,
expressed the truth of all philosophy; he duly
expounds the allegory of the *Aeneid* and finds
profitable wisdom for public and private life in the
Georgics and *Bucolics*. Like other medieval men

John knows that Ovid is, at times, a sound moralist and, like not all medieval men, he enjoys his smooth versification. John's favourite critical adjective is *ethicus*, and he emphasizes the moral teaching of Horace, Juvenal, Terence, and the rest. Seneca is almost a Christian. The Latin world held nothing greater than Cicero, who is cited along with the Fathers as a prime authority.

If we try to define the main principles explicit or implicit in John's writings, we see at once that they all grow out of that union of religious faith and classical culture which is called Christian humanism. John has literary taste and perception, but his chief interest is in the ethical value of the ancients, who supplement the Bible and the Fathers. Then his humanism is active and practical. He is himself an ecclesiastical administrator and publicist and he believes that learning and wisdom should be of service to society. The aim of education is "the knowledge of virtue which makes a good man." Grammar and logic are instruments, not ends in themselves. The study of *eloquentia* is not merely the cultivation of good Latin; eloquence is the medium through which alone man is able to use the reason God has given to him as distinct from the beasts. Here we may note that, although John reveres Aristotle as the master of logic, his heart is with the Christian Platonism fostered by the school of Chartres.

Finally, his whole philosophy rests on his belief in the universal authority of the church as the basis of the unity of civilization. It may be said that this harmonious equilibrium is artificial, that it depends on the absence of disturbing forces, but throughout its subsequent history, at any rate, humanism did not enjoy a sheltered life. It was, rather, on the battle front.

We come on to the fourteenth century, to a man who, if we allow for his poetic temperament and genius, is no less typical of the best culture and thought of his age. When we contemplate Petrarch, however, we see that the impulses of a nature more restless and complex than John's are perpetually at war with one another. Petrarch loves Laura, he loves his classical books, he loves his own art, and the world, and the adulation which the world so abundantly bestows. But he loves too the beauty of holiness, and his conscience is always tormenting him for his instability and want of will, which keep him in bondage to earthly desires. One could make Petrarch's inner struggle more vivid by thinking, say, of the young Matthew Arnold, though, after all, it is one of the ills that flesh and spirit are heir to in every age. Indeed the less intense Boccaccio had a similar struggle and achieved, with Petrarch's advice, an edifying and not too exacting compromise. Even Chaucer, who had no apparent difficulty in reconciling

4

conflicting claims in his private religion, could not do so in his greatest work of art.

Whatever conflict there may be between Petrarch's religion and the world, there is little between his religion and his love of the classics. With all the aesthetic sensitivity of a poet, he does not fail to stress the ethical and religious quality of the ancient authors. Seneca's moral teaching was close to that of Christianity. If Varro had been able to consult St. Augustine he would have become a great theologian. Virgil, with or without allegory—Petrarch has his sceptical moments—is the chief of poetic teachers. What Virgil is in poetry, or even more than that, Cicero is in prose. While Petrarch sees faults of character in the man, he puts Cicero the moralist and stylist on the throne he was to occupy for centuries:

You are well aware that from early boyhood of all the writers of all ages and of all races the one author whom I most admire and love is Cicero. . . . I am not afraid of being considered a poor Christian by declaring myself so much of a Ciceronian. To my knowledge, Cicero never wrote one word that would conflict with the principles proclaimed by Christ. If, perchance, his works contained anything contrary to Christ's doctrine, that one fact would be sufficient to destroy my belief in Cicero, and in Aristotle, too, and in Plato. . . . Christ is my God; Cicero, on the other hand, is the prince of the language I use. I grant you that these ideas are widely separated, but I deny that they are at conflict one with the other. . . . For, considering his noble and almost divine intellect, if Cicero had seen

Christ or had merely heard of His name, not only (in my opinion) would he have embraced the faith, but, with his incomparable eloquence, would most ably have spread the teachings of Christ.[1]

Petrarch's confessions, which are as unflattering as any honest self-portraiture is bound to be, should not lead us to undervalue his highest ideals and aspirations. Writers who insist on making Petrarch the first modern man—Renan's label has been more often repeated than examined—emphasize his worldly or "pagan" impulses and regard his frequent expressions of Christian piety, humility, and self-reproach as mainly conventional lipservice. Such a view is quite arbitrary prejudice. The important fact is not that Petrarch feels worldly longings but that he tries earnestly to resist them. Surely the name "Christian" is not reserved for those who never fall. Petrarch is more modern than John of Salisbury in his self-conscious and aristocratic enthusiasm for classical culture, in his critical appreciation of literary art, in his historical grasp of antiquity and its heroic figures— and symptoms of a general advance must not all be assigned to Petrarch's individuality—yet his humanism is unintelligible without his religious faith. We have seen something of his approach to his favourite classical authors, and he himself, by

<hr>

[1]*Petrarch's Letters to Classical Authors*, trans. M. E. Cosenza (University of Chicago Press, 1910), pp. 18-20; *Epistolae Familiares*, XXI. 10 (*Epistolae*, ed. G. Fracassetti [Florence, 1859-63], III, 85-7).

virtue of his moral works in Latin, was a Christian Cicero. If the first modern man can be imagined as reading the Fathers at all, he ought to have preferred Lactantius, or Erasmus' beloved Jerome —and Petrarch did like these—but the one who haunted his mind was Luther's teacher, Augustine, the saint tortured by the memory of his worldly sins. While Petrarch's own pangs of conscience are partly warranted, they are partly also the result of holding a too ascetic ideal of life—which is not one of the usual marks of modernity. As for his view of society at large, Petrarch averts his eyes from chaotic Italy to contemplate an ancient world under the *pax Romana*, moving toward the light of Christian revelation and Catholic unity.

Petrarch felt the need of Greek more acutely than John of Salisbury, although, through no fault of his own, he knew very little more. But one particular instinct, already apparent in John, has become much stronger in Petrarch, and it is significant both for his own age and for the future. That is his turning away from Aristotle, or rather from the medièval Aristotelians, to Plato. Petrarch had some knowledge of Plato in translation and he had absorbed the Platonic strain in Cicero and Augustine, but his sense of an elective affinity involved more than mere knowledge. By his time, indeed much earlier, we see the distinct emergence of that conflict which under different names and

different conditions has gone on ever since, the
conflict between religious or humanistic and irreligious scientific philosophies. The general broaden-
ing of intellectual horizons in the thirteenth century
in some vital ways enriched the classical revival of
the twelfth, but the immediately obvious mark
of the thirteenth century is the dominance of
scholasticism and the rise of new and insidious
enemies of Christian culture. When the successors
of Aquinas exposed the contradictions latent in
Thomism, separated reason and faith, and trans-
ferred theology to the province of the "irrational,"
they opened the way for that sceptical rationalism
which was to grow stronger in every age. Virtual
exclusion of spiritual problems from the field of
rational inquiry left nothing but the world of
nature outside man. Then there was the increasing
strength of the Averroists, followers of the Arabian
commentator on Aristotle, whose rationalistic
doctrines were quite positively anti-Christian.
When Petrarch attacked the Averroists and
scientists he was not merely beating the air and
betraying the ignorant prejudices of a literary man.
As Toffanin says, the Arabs had brought back the
science, but not the wisdom, of the Greeks.
Petrarch could see that the new modes of thought
were destructive of Christian faith, ethics, and
culture, and he was reasserting the universal claims
of religious and humane values. That is a major

reason for his exaltation of Cicero and Plato; they
are on the side of the angels and the Aristotelians
are not. (The later debt of science to Renaissance
Platonism is another story.) Thus the humanism
of Petrarch and his successors is not merely one
more stage in that long process, the recovery of
classical culture. Its character and direction are
sharpened and concentrated by the necessity of
fighting philosophies which deny all that Christian
humanism stands for.

Here we may observe a very misleading idea
which is to be met in modern writers of all kinds.
It is assumed as an unquestionable fact that
humanism and related words signify a turning
from heaven to earth, from medieval theology and
otherworldliness to this mundane world which the
classics have taught men to enjoy. One would not
say that such motives do not appear, but one
would say also, first, that it is a peculiar definition
of Christianity which makes the enjoyment of all
earthly and literary pleasures unchristian, and,
secondly, that really unchristian neo-paganism is
a very minor element in comparison with the
positive Christian humanism I am trying to describe. Humanism in the Renaissance normally
means Christian faith in alliance with God-given
reason, which is the most human faculty in man.
Humanism is that way of life and thought which
keeps man in union with God and above the

biological level. It opposes both the irreligious
scientific rationalism which would separate man
from the divine, and the ethical or unethical
naturalism—often the eldest child of rationalism—
which would link him with the beasts. Common
humanistic labels for these two sets of enemies are
"Averroists" and "Epicureans."

Serious humanists could not well defend their
house if it was divided against itself, if the fusion
of classical culture with religion were not felt as a
living reality. Of the multitude of utterances on
the great theme of reconciliation only a few typical
examples can be quoted. Without Christ, Petrarch
repeats, learning can never bring happiness; as
Augustine, following Plato, had affirmed, "If
wisdom is God, through whom all things are made
(as divine authority and truth declare), the true
philosopher is a lover of God."   For Coluccio
Salutati, the chief Italian humanist of the generation after Petrarch, "Humane studies are bound
up together; and the study of divinity is bound up
with them, so that a true and complete knowledge
of the one cannot be had without the other."
Humane studies, says Leonardo Bruni, are those
which have to do with life and conduct, those
which form a good man, that is, the works of the
ancient philosophers, poets, orators, and historians;
scientific and professional knowledge, though good
in itself, does not teach how to live rightly. Much

of Christian humanism is embodied in Ficino's
assertion that nothing pertains more to man than
discussions of the soul. The devout Ficino took
as his life-work the reconciling of Plato and
Plotinus with Christianity, and he and Pico della
Mirandola encouraged each other in their effort
to propagate Christian Platonism and to defend
true faith and piety against Averroistic heresy and
Epicurean impiety. The humanistic quarrel with
the scientists Ficino summed up concisely: Aristotle deals with the nature of things, he, Ficino,
with the nature of men.

Apart from their spiritual godfather, Petrarch,
all these humanists belong to Florence, and in
spite of particular differences they constitute, in
comparison with other shifting groups and individuals, a fairly united front and a continuous
tradition. Their humanism is more or less strongly
Christian and ethical, with Stoic, Aristotelian, or,
above all, Platonic emphasis. It is also strongly
practical—except in the medieval Petrarch—and
makes active civic responsibility an essential part
of the good life. More fully than any other Italian
tradition this Florentine humanism passed into
early Tudor England. The main element trans-
mitted was a Christian Platonism of ethical,
educational, and political solidity; it was only in
the Italianate Elizabethan age that the less
substantial religion of beauty won poetical cur-

rency. It may be said that the Florentine fusion
of Christianity and Platonism was itself a nebulous
wraith, but it was a wraith which has been an
alluring ideal throughout modern civilization. It
may also be said that these Florentines are in-
adequately representative of Italian humanism at
large; yet, if a wider survey brought in sceptics
and neo-pagans, it would add many sober
Christians too.

The Christian tradition behind Christian
humanism needs no comment. The great source
of the humanistic tradition is Cicero. Thirty
years ago Paul Elmer More made a remark which
in his later days he might not have endorsed.
"I question," he said, "whether Cicero, while he
certainly represents what is more enduring, has
not been also, actually and personally, as dynamic
an influence in civilisation as St. Paul, though the
noise, no doubt, and the tumult, have been around
the latter." That claim cannot be substantiated
in a few paragraphs but some grounds for it can
be indicated. In the first place, the philosophic
orator and statesman was the exemplar of Roman
civic consciousness and the active life. The
Ciceronian ideal, when recognized, conflicted with
the ideal of monastic contemplation and did not
gain ground until the later Middle Ages, but for
the humanists of the Renaissance it was a potent
inspiration. The conception of Dante as the

citizen-poet, which we take for granted, was first
set forth, as Hans Baron has shown, by Leonardo
Bruni, who was writing in the civic spirit of the
De Oratore. The same treatise left a strong impress
upon Castiglione's great book. As for Cicero the
philosopher and writer, his vast and many-sided
authority was exerted throughout the medieval as
well as the later period. Though some of his works
contributed to the current of Renaissance scepticism, in the main he was a buttress of orthodoxy.
From Cicero's voluminous moral treatises I can
cite only a few reminders of his humanistic outlook
and ethical doctrine. There is that utterance in
the *De Republica* which Lactantius thought well-
nigh inspired, that morality is founded on the
eternal law of right reason written in every human
heart. The watchword of the humanists is *sapientia,*
which Cicero defines in the *De Officiis* not as mere
mundane prudence but as "the knowledge of things
human and divine, which is concerned also with
the bonds of union between gods and men and the
relations of man to man." As a fuller definition of
Renaissance humanism we might take this passage
from the same work: [2]

And it is no mean manifestation of Nature and Reason
that man is the only animal that has a feeling for order,
for propriety, for moderation in word and deed. And so

---

[2]*De Officiis*, i.4.14, 5.15 (Loeb Classical Library). See also *ibid.*,
i.43.153.

no other animal has a sense of beauty, loveliness, harmony in the visible world; and Nature and Reason, extending the analogy of this from the world of sense to the world of spirit, find that beauty, consistency, order are far more to be maintained in thought and deed, and the same Nature and Reason are careful to do nothing in an improper or unmanly fashion, and in every thought and deed to do or think nothing capriciously.

It is from these elements that is forged and fashioned that moral goodness which is the subject of this inquiry. . . .

You see here, Marcus, my son, the very form and as it were the face of Moral Goodness; "and if," as Plato says, "it could be seen with the physical eye, it would awaken a marvellous love of wisdom." But all that is morally right rises from some one of four sources: it is concerned either (1) with the full perception and intelligent development of the true; or (2) with the conservation of organized society, with rendering to every man his due, and with the faithful discharge of obligations assumed; or (3) with the greatness and strength of a noble and invincible spirit; or (4) with the orderliness and moderation of everything that is said and done, wherein consist temperance and self-control.

Although Cicero moulded the pattern of prose in most modern languages, his fundamental influence, from the Fathers down, was of the kind suggested by these excerpts. Guided by the natural light of reason, the Greeks' and his own, Cicero had brought moral philosophy, *sapientia*, to the threshold of Christianity. It was Cicero who led the brilliant worldling, Augustine, to God. It was Cicero, along with such a partial disciple as

Augustine, who led Petrarch and Ficino and others to Plato and Christian Platonism. When Cicero is almost deified as a moral teacher, a teacher of unique urbanity and sweetness and light, imitation of his style and the minute study of rhetoric appear in their proper perspective. We must not consider Renaissance Ciceronianism as merely a stylistic fad justly satirized by Erasmus and justly denounced by Bacon. Imitation of Ciceronian Latin for its own sake did sometimes run to absurd excess, but that outbreak of neoclassical measles was confined to a small number of men. By far the great majority of Renaissance humanists think of good Latin as John of Salisbury had thought of it: through eloquence alone man is able to use that faculty of reason which God has given to him as distinct from the beasts. The good orator or writer must be a good man. Eloquence, Cicero had said, is articulate wisdom; without wisdom it is a very dangerous thing. Such sentiments are echoed, with more or less Christian emphasis, from Petrarch to Pico, from Erasmus to Sturm. While in matters of faith the modern world is on a different plane from the ancient, yet in many respects antiquity has much to teach us, and if we wish to have another golden age we must re-create it. In the Latin language, says Valla, are comprised all the disciplines which are worthy of a free man. Who, he asks, are the men who have been great

philosophers, orators, jurists, in short, great
authors? Only those who have striven to speak
well. If we will only strive heroically enough, the
universal Roman speech, and along with it every
branch of learning, will revive and flourish in its
old splendour. Finally, since Erasmus' satire on
Ciceronianism has been mentioned, let us have
Erasmus' real feeling about Cicero himself:[3]

Whatsoever is pious, and conduces to good manners,
ought not to be called profane. The first place must indeed
be given to the authority of the Scriptures; but neverthe-
less, I sometimes find some things said or written by the
ancients, nay, even by the heathens, nay, by the poets
themselves, so chastely, so holily, and so divinely, that I
cannot persuade myself but that when they wrote them
they were divinely inspired; and perhaps the spirit of Christ
diffuses itself farther than we imagine; and that there are
more saints than we have in our catalogue. To confess
freely among friends, I cannot read Tully "On Old Age,"
"On Friendship," his "Offices," or his "Tusculan Questions,"
without kissing the book, and veneration for that divine
soul. . . .

Although all Tully's books of philosophy seem to
breathe out something divine, yet that treatise on old age,
that he wrote in old age, seems to me to be according to
the Greek proverb, "the song of the dying swan." I was
reading it today, and these words pleasing me above the
rest, I got them by heart: "Should it please God to give
me a grant to begin my life again from my very cradle,
and once more to run over the course of my years I
have lived, I would not upon any terms accept of it. Nor

---

[3]"The Religious Banquet," *Colloquies* (Bailey's translation).

would I, having in a manner finished my race, run it over again from the starting-place to the goal. For what pleasure has this life in it? Nay, rather, what pain has it not? But if there were not, there would be undoubtedly in it satiety or trouble. I am not for bewailing my past life as a great many, and learned men too, have done, nor do I repent that I have lived, because I have lived so that I am satisfied I have not lived in vain. And when I leave this life, I leave it as an inn, and not as a place of abode. For Nature has given us our bodies as an inn to lodge in, and not to dwell in. O glorious day that will be when I shall leave this rabble rout and defilements of the world behind me, to go to that society and world of spirits!" Thus far out of Cato. What could be spoken more divinely by a Christian? I wish all the discourses of our monks, even with their holy virgins, were such as the dialogue of this aged pagan with the pagan youths of his time.

And I must add Erasmus' comment, in the same colloquy, on Plato's account of the death of Socrates, for nothing in Renaissance writing is closer to the heart of Christian humanism:

Indeed, it was a wonderful elevation of mind in a man that knew not Christ nor the Holy Scriptures. And therefore I can scarce forbear, when I read such things of such men, but cry out: "*Sancte Socrates, ora pro nobis.*"

To sum up, as Virgil's career is the ideal model for the Renaissance poet, Cicero is the great example of the philosopher in politics, of enlightened public service; and Ciceronian *eloquentia* is the outward mark of an inward spiritual grace, of learned piety and urbanity. It represents the religious and cultural orthodoxy of an international and aristocratic classical discipline, and it is the practical instrument and the intellectual symbol of the unity of Christian civilization.

We have glanced at some typical humanists from the twelfth century onward, and instead of reciting a generalized list of the unchanging elements in the humanistic creed it might be better to say a little more of the man who supremely embodied and enriched the tradition. Erasmus was perhaps the most influential teacher in the history of modern European culture. The delicate and fastidious features pictured by Holbein suggest, as a scholar has remarked, that Erasmus might have been descended from a line of maiden aunts, but, in spite of poor health, draughty houses, bad beer, and frequent migrations, he accomplished an enormous amount of work. It would take a long time to catalogue his original books, his compilations, and his editions of patristic and classical writers, not to mention the great body of letters. That immense and varied output was inspired by a single aim, the propagation of Christian humanism, of a purified Catholicism in alliance with the moral wisdom and rational culture of antiquity. Erasmus has no interest in anything which does not minister to truly religious and humane values. He damns scientists and superstitious zealots, literary pedants and illiterate

monks, barren logicians and godless prelates. While
Erasmus owed something to the boldly critical
Valla, he owed much more to John Colet. When
Erasmus first visited England his whole nature
expanded in the sunshine of that brilliant group
of early humanists, but it seems to have been
Colet who opened the eyes of the discontented and
restless scholastic to the prime need of spread-
ing the simple gospel of Christ.

With all his wit and urbane culture, Erasmus
did not pursue learning for learning's sake. "All
studies, philosophy, rhetoric, are followed for this
one object, that we may know Christ and honour
Him. This is the end of all learning and eloquence."
To Budé, a sincere Christian but a great scholar
of the pure type, Erasmus wrote: "You have
preferred to be understood by the learned, I, if I
can, by the many; your aim is to conquer, mine
to teach or persuade." Erasmus might use his
Greek to translate Euripides, or even Lucian—who
perhaps taught him the irony he has been said to
have brought back into European literature—but
his great object was to return to the unadulterated
fountains of Christianity in the Fathers and above
all in the New Testament. His prayer was that
the New Testament might be translated into all
languages, so as to be known "not merely by the
Scotch and Irish, but even by the Turks and
Saracens," that scriptural passages might be in

the mind of the farmer following his plough and
the weaver at his loom.

Of the extent and the nature of Erasmus' love
of the classics it is needless to speak. We have
seen how he felt toward Cicero and Plato, and
seen enough, perhaps, to understand his ethical
attitude. All the traditional ideals of Christian
humanism appear in Erasmus in clearer relief than
they ever had appeared before, because of his
exceptional literary power, single-hearted purpose,
and vast influence. To him as to his predecessors
the Bible, the Fathers, and the classics together
offered, not a nostalgic dream of unattainable
perfection, but a working ideal of a universal
state in which reason and the will of God should
prevail. In an age of violent nationalism Erasmus
pleaded for the international brotherhood of
Christian virtue and good letters. War he denounced as the occupation of savages. Religion
and culture, he insisted, need peace and must
create peace. Given time, education can work
miracles, in the individual and in the world at
large. The reformation of the church must be
accomplished by gradual enlightenment, not by
force.

Luther's revolt meant the destruction of all
that Erasmus held most dear, of the cause to which
he had given his life. Very early the two men
gauged each other accurately, and the course of

events confirmed their increasingly hostile judgments. Erasmus was attacked by Catholics because, as a loyal son of the church and its chief
writer, he did not formally assail Luther, and he
was attacked by Protestants because, as the
satirist who had awakened Europe to the need of
reform, he did not ally himself with the militant
reformer. Erasmus' neutrality has often been
called cowardice, although, as Professor E. K.
Rand once remarked, it takes some courage to
pursue one's work in the middle of No Man's
Land. When Erasmus did finally speak out against
Luther, it was in a treatise on the freedom of the
will. If this seemed an oddly academic subject to
propound at such a time, Luther knew better; he
said Erasmus had taken him by the throat. The
episode dramatizes the fundamental contrast between the fervent Augustinian monk, who denies
freewill and maintains predestination, total depravity, and salvation by grace alone, and the half-
Pelagian humanist whose hopes for religious and
cultural betterment are based on faith in man's
rational self-direction and essential goodness.
Erasmus would not admit that desperate diseases
needed desperate remedies, and his tragedy was
the tragedy of humanists in all ages. For the
moment, at least, the intense and narrow-minded
zealot usually overpowers the sane and cultivated
conservative who has none of the prejudice of

passion and none of its force. Luther could cite
the classics on occasion, but in his world of despair
and ecstasy there was no middle level for *sapientia*
and *humanitas*.

The antagonism between Luther and Erasmus
does not need to be emphasized, but since we shall
encounter again the pessimism inherent in evangelical Protestantism and the optimism inherent in
Christian humanism, I may put some typical
utterances side by side. This is Luther:

God has promised certainly His grace to the humbled:
that is, to the self-deploring and despairing. But a man
cannot be thoroughly humbled, until he comes to know
that his salvation is utterly beyond his own powers,
counsel, endeavours, will, and works, and absolutely
depending on the will, counsel, pleasure, and work of
another, that is, of God only.

And this is Erasmus:

I affirm that, as the instinct of the dog is to hunt, of the
bird to fly, of the horse to gallop, so the natural bent of
man is to philosophy and right conduct. As every creature
most readily learns that for which it is created, therefore
will man, with but slight effort, be brought to follow that
to which Nature has given him so strong an instinct,
namely, excellence, but on one condition: that Nature be
reinforced by the wise energy of the educator. . . . What
is the proper nature of man? Surely it is to live the life of
reason, for reason is the peculiar prerogative of man.

And I must add another passage from a tract in
which Erasmus asks how man, being what he is,
can make war like a beast:

Nature hath endued man with knowledge of liberal sciences and a fervent desire of knowledge: which thing as it doth most specially withdraw man's wit from all beastly wildness, so hath it a special grace to get and knit together love and friendship. For I dare boldly say, that neither affinity nor yet kindred doth bind the minds of men together with straiter and surer bands of amity, than doth the fellowship of them that be learned in good letters and honest studies. And above all this, Nature hath divided among men by a marvellous variety the gifts as well of the soul as of the body. . . . Finally, she hath endowed man with a spark of a godly mind: so that though he see no reward, yet of his own courage he delighteth to do every man good. . . . Moreover, God hath ordained man in this world, as it were the very image of Himself, to the intent, that he, as it were a god on earth, should provide for the wealth of all creatures.

There is no need of summarizing what has been said so often about the general character of continental humanism. The briefest account of it, from the twelfth century to the early sixteenth, reveals a creed and a programme in which the major articles remain constant. Whatever qualifications a larger survey might compel one to make, they would not alter the main conclusion, that the classical humanism of the Renaissance was fundamentally medieval and fundamentally Christian.

III *English Humanism*

MODERN HISTORIANS, while making the spirit
of the Renaissance spread from Italy over the
rest of Europe, have regularly contrasted the
aesthetic, irreligious neo-paganism of the South
with the sober Christian piety of the North. The
fundamental change that humanism underwent in
crossing the Alps was presumably due to the
invincible moral constitution of the northern
nations, which were profoundly stimulated by an
impulse they rejected. Such a view, so congenial
to the Nordic and especially the Anglo-Saxon
belief that the Latin peoples are inevitably immoral, has its measure of truth, but even our brief
glance at Italian humanism may serve as a qualifi-
cation. We have seen something of the religious,
ethical, and civic motives of Florentine humanism
in particular, and all that we can safely assert is
that such motives were in the North even more
pure and predominant than they were in Italy as
a whole. If northern humanism grew up largely
in the service of the Reformation, we should
remember that much of the energy of Italian
humanism was devoted to the support or the
revival of medieval religious orthodoxy. When we
read in Bacon and Milton that the Reformation,
with its appeal to ancient authority, brought about
the classical Renaissance, we may say that these

men, lacking our long perspective, put the cart before the horse, yet their view is much nearer the truth than that of modern historians who consider the Renaissance essentially irreligious.

The real character of English humanism did not definitely emerge until the end of the fifteenth century, though it might have been predicted much earlier. Nearly all the Englishmen who went to Italy to study or had connections with Italian humanists were churchmen, and the increasing strength of the classical revival did not fundamentally alter their religious habits of life and thought. They sometimes show a veneer of literary aestheticism, but it is only a veneer. Whatever neo-paganism flourished in Italy, these men did not seek it or acquire it. Most of the fifteenth-century English travellers came home with their books and lecture-notes and planted themselves in their ecclesiastical furrows, to make the earth fruitful or, perhaps, merely to vegetate. In the early fifteenth century Poggio was able to sneer at barbarous Englishmen. Some eighty years later Erasmus rejoices in being welcomed by a group of English humanists which has no superior in Europe, and Aldus recognizes, in the person of Linacre, the international authority of English scholarship. We cannot take account here of the early phases of humanism in England—they have been illuminated by Professor Schirmer—but logic as well as history would prevent us from regarding as a sudden phenomenon the appearance of that distinguished circle which included Grocyn, Colet, More, Linacre, Latimer, Lily, and others. And these names indicate the character of English humanism in its first maturity, a thoroughly religious and ethical character which had its Catholic and Protestant phases and then passed into such divergent channels as learned puritanism and Cambridge Platonism.

Except More, who early in life took Pico as his model, all of these men studied in Italy, and Italy only confirmed and ripened a humanism more positively religious and practical than that of their somewhat shadowy predecessors. The oldest of the group, William Grocyn, seemed to younger admirers the very incarnation of Christian humanism. Though a theologian of the old school, Grocyn came to accept Valla's proof that "Dionysius the Areopagite" was not a writer of the apostolic age. From Italy Colet brought back something of Savonarola's ascetic rigour and a new or enlarged knowledge of the Christian Platonism of Ficino and Pico. If Italian humanism taught Colet an historical approach to the Epistles of St. Paul, it— and a nearer view of the Papacy—also fortified his zeal for a simplified theology, for the inward reformation of the universal church and its individual members on the pattern of Christ Himself.

Lily was the first head of Colet's school of St.
Paul's. Linacre, while less actively devout than
Colet and More, was a great exemplar of both
philological and scientific humanism. Almost all
the men of this circle were able Grecians as well
as Latinists, and most of them, like Erasmus,
studied Greek in order to have the key to the New
Testament, to drink of the unadulterated fountain
of Christianity. Linacre's motto was also *"ad
fontes."* His Greek scholarship (like that of
Rabelais some years later) was applied to purifying
the great works of classical science and medicine
from medieval accretions.

One topic must be emphasized, though briefly.
We cannot over-estimate the importance of the
Platonic strain in English humanism. In two
groups of men it manifests itself with special
power, in Colet, Erasmus, More, and Elyot in the
early sixteenth century, and in the Cambridge
Platonists in the middle of the seventeenth; in the
intervening period the irrigating stream had not
dried up. This Platonism was, of course, eclectic,
drawn, in varying proportions, from Plato and
Plotinus, Augustine and Dionysius, Ficino and
Pico. It appeared in diverse forms, in political and
educational thought, in truly religious mysticism
and in amatory pseudo-mysticism, in doctrines of
rational ethics and of supra-rational poetic inspiration. But everywhere it had a fertilizing, broaden-

ing, and sweetening influence. In the history of thought one could name many narrow, dogmatic Aristotelians; it would be hard to name a narrow, dogmatic Platonist. In England, in an age of puritan strictness, Platonism gave to rules of Christian piety and virtue a rational sanity and an idealistic ardour which inspired not only religious thinkers but poets like Spenser and Milton. In an age of sectarian conflict it made for charity and tolerance, for the belief that, as a living Platonist has said, the grace of God is not distributed denominationally.

Much has been made, by early and modern commentators, of the decline of learning in England in the middle third of the sixteenth century. Professor R. W. Chambers, elaborating a theory set forth by J. S. Phillimore, has vehemently argued that Henry VIII was the ruthless destroyer of a rich culture, that English humanism was typically personified in More, that More's execution was a blow which paralysed it for generations, and that "it was not till the days of Bentley that classical scholarship recovered in England the position it held in the days of Erasmus, before Henry axed it." I have tried to show, in the *University of Toronto Quarterly* (VII, 162), that these notions will not bear scrutiny, and the facts cannot be rehearsed now. It can only be said briefly that some setback to learning was inevitable during a period when the official religion of the country changed so often, when university men were at the centre of religious and political controversy, when scholarly freedom and security might give place to dismissal, exile, or imprisonment. But, at least in regard to the numerical decline of university students, the lamentations of early and modern historians can be convicted of rhetorical excess; and, while the loss of morale must have been serious, that too can be exaggerated. The fifth decade of the century, which has often been regarded as the dark age, was after all the one period in English history before Bentley when classical studies in an English university were a matter of international fame, when Sir John Cheke taught Cambridge and King Edward Greek. Then, after the short and troubled reigns of Edward and Mary, came the accession of Elizabeth, the return of the Marian exiles, and the beginning of strife between Anglican and puritan. All along, of course, English Catholicism created unceasing difficulties. When such disturbance was a permanent fact of the Tudor world, we may wonder that humanism did not suffer more than it appears to have done.

But our concern must be with the spiritual and intellectual quality of humanism, not with its history. The great change from Catholicism to Protestantism meant that the older humanistic ideal of a universal church as the channel of a purified universal faith gave way to a more national outlook on national questions. That Cheke and Ascham are of smaller stature than Colet and More, Mr. Chambers would doubtless explain by saying that they were not angels but Anglicans. Although we should not ascribe all differences in individual character and endowment to a general change in religion, we might, without pressing the parallel, put Colet and Ascham beside Newman and Kingsley. There is something of Kingsley in the simple, sturdy, English faith of the prefatory verses to Ascham's *Toxophilus:*

> Reioyse Englande, be gladde and merie,
> Trothe ouercommeth thyne enemyes all.
> The Scot, the Frencheman, the Pope, and heresie,
> Overcommed by Trothe, haue had a fall:
> Sticke to the Trothe, and euermore thou shall
> Through Christ, King Henry, the Boke and the Bowe
> All maner of enemies, quite ouerthrowe.

While in the middle decades of the century Truth, as embodied in the Church of England, is something of a chameleon, the Protestant humanists, like their Catholic predecessors, are men of sober piety—though it has been observed that Ascham's censure of dicing betrays a rather minute knowledge of technique. If Ascham has a less intense and less philosophic spirituality than Colet, he only reveals more clearly the plain moral puritanism which was a large element in the Catholic divine. On the other hand, while Colet had been afraid of ancient pagan literature, Ascham lived with the classics and constantly celebrated them as a treasury of wisdom second only to the Bible.

For in their fervently didactic faith in the classical authors as the supreme guides, outside of revelation, to life and conduct as well as the arts of expression, the Protestant humanists shared a traditional orthodoxy which was an even more universal bond than Catholicism. The first formal defence of poetry written in the Tudor age, that of the Catholic Sir Thomas Elyot, is essentially the same in spirit as John of Salisbury's. The function of poets is to teach, and even Plautus and Terence, Ovid and Martial, have good counsel mixed with their licentious matter. Ascham is never weary of proclaiming the creed he holds with his friend and preceptor, Cheke:

These books be not many, nor long, nor rude in speech, nor mean in matter; but next the majesty of God's holy word, most worthy for a man, the lover of learning and honesty, to spend his life in. Yea, I have heard worthy Mr. Cheke many times say; I would have a good student pass and journey through all authors both Greek and Latin. But he that will dwell in these few books only; first, in God's holy Bible, and then join with it Tully in Latin, Plato, Aristotle, Xenophon, Isocrates, and Demosthenes in Greek, must needs prove an excellent man.

One need not multiply documentary proofs of the indissoluble marriage of virtue and good letters.

And while the great end of education is virtuous discipline, that does not mean indifference to the aesthetic appeal of ancient literature; it does mean emphasis on moral and philosophic substance, on values immediately applicable to life. Of much modern study of the classics, and literature in general, we might say what has been said of the New Testament, that we make up for not believing in Christ by admiring His style. In the sixteenth century, veneration for the ancients as a superior race of beings might, of course, lead to slavish subservience, but that was only the occasional defect of a saving faith in high standards. If we want to be like the ancients, devout humanists said, we must imitate even their gestures, and, rightly understood, that is not an ignoble creed. We have seen that continental humanists, from Petrarch to Sturm, echoed Cicero's doctrine that eloquence is nothing but articulate wisdom, and that eloquence without wisdom is a weapon in the hand of a madman. The same faith in good Latin, and the same warning, are repeated in England not merely by a professional classicist like Ascham but by a divine like Thomas Becon. Good Latin, as the instrument of God-given reason, is the symbol of religious, ethical, and social solidarity. When we think of the Renaissance humanist's limitless faith in the possibilities of education, we may remember among other things that that faith was not annually sapped by the spectacle of alumni reunions.

The broad aim of Tudor humanism was training in virtue and good letters; the practical aim was training for the active Christian life, especially public life. For humanism was not only religious, it was also both aristocratic and utilitarian. The mere title of Elyot's book, *The Governour*, indicates its object. It continues the long tradition of European treatises on the education of a Christian prince, a tradition carried on in many similar documents down to Milton's *Of Education*. And we do not need to limit ourselves to pedagogical works, for the same motive inspires the heroic romances of Sidney and Spenser. This is a basic element in Tudor humanism which Phillimore and Mr. Chambers apparently do not understand. The idea that the failure of later Tudor England to produce great works of pure scholarship is a mark of arrested development betrays a misconception of the vital spirit of English humanism. More had no desire to rival Scaliger, nor did Erasmus—if we may count him as partly English—envy the reputation of Budé. Erasmus and More and their followers did not investigate the coinage or the grammar of the ancients, they sought to make the rational wisdom of antiquity supplement the teaching of Christ. *The Praise of Folly* and *Utopia*, *The Governour* and *The Scholemaster* remain living

books. All the English humanists, like the
majority of continental ones, regarded classical
learning as a means, not an end, and their energies
were given to education. They wished to produce
citizens and statesmen, not scholars. It was these
Tudor humanists who established what was to be
the ruling motive of English classical study down
to the days of "the Jowett mind." From More to
Milton the writings of English humanists are
chiefly on public affairs, education, and religion.
William Cecil might have remained a college don
and crowned his life with an edition of Aristotle's
Politics; instead he applied ancient wisdom (not
without help from Machiavelli) to practical states-
manship. Classical scholars pure and simple have
always been rare accidents in England. A. E.
Housman believed that the function of a classical
scholar in our time was the emending of texts,
preferably of bad poets. That was not the belief
of More and Elyot and Cheke and Ascham and
Sir Thomas Smith and Thomas Wilson. If Housman belongs, in learning and temper, to the
tradition of J. C. Scaliger, the modern descendants
of these Tudor humanists are men like Dean Inge
and Gilbert Murray, Sir Alfred Zimmern and Sir
Ronald Storrs.

We might think Christian humanism was so
firmly rooted as a working faith, as a final educational and moral discipline, that nothing, not

even religious and political unrest, could shake it for ages to come. But I wish in the rest of this hour to review some of the causes, internal and external, which led to what may be called the break-up of the Renaissance synthesis. In using such a phrase I do not mean, of course, that Christian humanism was ever completely dominant or that it was ever completely extinguished. Yet in the sixteenth century humanism is a relatively universal and recognizably definite frame of religious and cultural philosophy, a tower of strength which has many zealous defenders and, in England, few formidable enemies. It is, to change metaphors, the one great highway along which men march toward the city of God. In the seventeenth century, if we look at the moulders and representatives of the new age, Christian humanism is no longer so universal or so definitely recognizable. The tower is assailed or undermined by avowed or unconscious enemies. The one straight road has split into many paths, and while some men confidently proclaim that this or that one is the certain way, others hang back in troubled bewilderment. The Christian humanist of the Middle Ages or the Renaissance knew the inward things essential for the good life and what he did not know about the outer or even the inner world did not matter. For the seventeenth-century man both the outer and the inner world have become oppressively vast and dark, and the great question is "What do I know?" Such a condensed contrast only means that various disruptive forces, while in operation centuries earlier, have in England become conspicuous in the seventeenth century. Most of those forces we have already encountered in passing, but some must be recapitulated now, with the inadequacy which attends any effort to describe ages of civilization in half an hour.

In the first place Christian humanism, which depended so much on the personality of its exponents, might suffer from internal decay and dry rot. There was then, as always, the danger that the official custodians of *litterae humaniores* might forget the spirit for the letter, might allow a gospel of life to become a classroom routine, that the study of virtue and literature might give way to grammar and flagellation—though one may prefer the old tradition at its worst to the progressive modernism which has banished both flagellation and grammar.

The classical discipline had many groups of external enemies. Puritans echoed some of the Fathers and their many Catholic successors in denouncing pagan writings. Puritanism also helped to swell and exacerbate controversial theology and to make Hebrew a rival of Latin and Greek. Logic, that old foe of the classics, had been given a fresh lease of life by Peter Ramus, and theologians and

rhetoricians delighted in the exercise of their
handy new tools. Then the classics bulked large
in general attacks on academic and liberal education. The aristocratic humanist creed had to
contend, as it has contended ever since, with the
rising tide of democratic and practical sentiment
which favoured popular and professional training.
The man of action and the man of the world
despised the "unsuccessful" student's contem-
plative incapacity and lack of polish. The cause
of humanism suffered from the poverty and social
humiliation which was the lot of many scholars and
teachers.

These various and important factors are too obvious for comment and we may go on to some more
inward problems confronting Christian humanism.
That humanism, as I have repeated so often, was a
medieval fusion of classical wisdom with Christian
faith, and the only real change in later times was
that the classical element, philosophically and
aesthetically, became a less inferior partner. But
now the Christian faith and the Christian church
were no longer the simple universal unity they had
been for John of Salisbury or Petrarch or even
Erasmus. Neither the Reformation nor the Coun-
ter-Reformation had much room for a saving
remnant of cultivated moderates who seemed little
better than Laodiceans. Many men who have
loved God have burned their fellow men, but few

who have loved letters have done so. The strong anti-cultural forces in both reformations meant that the purely religious spirit of early Christianity had finally won the day, that the classical Renaissance had only retarded for a while the triumph of St. Paul and Tertullian over Plato and Cicero, of Savonarola and Loyola and Luther and Calvin over Erasmus. Among Catholics of Tudor England the Hellenism and humanism of More and his circle were quite exceptional; Catholics for the most part clung to the old learning and fought against the new. The Protestantism of the Protestant Reformation was likewise opposed to humanism. Multiplying sects and parties, with their intolerance and frequent violence, did not share the ideal of a liberal, aristocratic, and international orthodoxy of sweetness and light. Lutheran and Calvinist dogmas were incompatible with the humanistic doctrine of the self-governing reason and dignity of man. The evangelical conception of religious "experience" was not what Erasmus or Milton understood by imitation of Christ. And besides the mass of more or less orthodox Calvinists there were religious groups and individuals of a kind Calvin himself attacked, those antinomian mystics who were guided by their inner light—a light which to nervous statesmen looked decidedly red. Lastly, classical humanism might suffer from both learned and unlearned champions of devout ignorance who denied the validity of all human knowledge.

Thus within the pale of religion itself, in the later sixteenth and earlier seventeenth centuries, the conditions which engendered and fostered Christian humanism have greatly changed. Universality and unity have given place to multiplicity and conflict. What, then, of the fact that many leaders of the Reformation in all countries were genuine humanists? They could be both because, consciously or not, they achieved a compromise. Their rational and ethical Christianity accepted classical humanism as a natural helpmate. In England the established church has from the beginning been the happy and comfortable home of those who, to employ a useful distinction made by one of Hardy's rustics, are "good, but not religious-good," who are Christians without "enthusiasm," and are too sane and cultivated to be damned by a sane and cultivated Anglican Deity. Fortunately the seventeenth century contained a number of men who kept open the *via media* between angry extremists, and whose moderate principles owed not a little to the humane and stabilizing power of the classical tradition.

Christian humanism had strong enemies outside religion. The scholastic synthesis of Christian faith and classical reason had been a creed for the few; the mass of medieval people took religion on simpler terms. And, through the pressure of forces from within and without, the Thomistic synthesis had not maintained for long its original character and balance. The humanistic synthesis was an aristocratic orthodoxy like early scholasticism, but a synthesis less subtly metaphysical and theological and more humane, literary, and utilitarian. It might be said, as I suggested before, that this Christian humanism was an artificial harmony predestined to be upset as soon as medieval ways of thought were outgrown, that its two scales depended on authority and their equilibrium on the absence or weakness of modern critical rationalism. But in granting that one must grant, whether to the credit or the discredit of the race, that medieval ways of thought lasted, powerfully, a very long time; the explorations of reason are circumscribed—or, some might say with equal truth, are inspired—by the same premises for Hooker as for Aquinas. And perhaps one is not bound to grant that Christian humanism was only the product of a naïve and immature phase of civilization which has no meaning for the modern world.

The two great philosophic enemies of religion and morality, and hence of Christian humanism, were sceptical and naturalistic doctrines. Even within the scholastic tradition the early divorce between reason and faith opened the way for those two extreme positions of the Renaissance, anti-Christian rationalism and anti-rational fideism. In the thirteenth and fourteenth centuries Aristotle had been the patron saint not only of scholastic theology and ethics but of irreligious rationalism and naturalism. In the fifteenth and sixteenth centuries, notably at the University of Padua, the doctrines of the Aristotelian commentators were further developed and propagated, and they were now strongly reinforced by increased knowledge of ancient sceptics, from Lucretius to Lucian. Even Cicero, another patron saint of orthodoxy, was, on the strength of the *De Natura Deorum* and *De Divinatione*, constantly invoked by rationalists. In the sixteenth century, and especially in England, religion and ethics, politics and economics, were inseparably united, and on all fronts Tudor humanism formed a solid bulwark of orthodox thought. While on the continent, in spite of the Inquisition and the Sorbonne, sceptical ideas circulated pretty freely—Pomponazzi and Vicomercato enjoyed the protection of cardinals—in England, whatever some men's private thinking or behaviour might be, public utterances were all of one kind. It is not till the end of the century that we encounter Ralegh's "school of atheism"—which was not atheistical—and such young rebels as Marlowe and Donne. Up till then we infer the knowledge of heretical doctrines mainly from the frequent attacks on them.

In the defence of orthodoxy against scepticism or naturalism or both, the humanists took a large part. The roll might begin with More's versatile brother-in-law, John Rastell, who, in replying to an attack on the dogma of purgatory, chose to defend the existence of God and purgatory and the immortality of the soul on purely rational grounds, without recourse to Scripture. Sir John Cheke apparently introduced a new word into English by describing as "atheists" men who followed their passions and cared not for God, heaven, or hell. The part of *The Scholemaster* most familiar to the modern reader is the invective against Italian atheism and wickedness; Ascham names Machiavelli. In the fashionable *Euphues*, which might be called a godchild of *The Scholemaster*, a whole section is given to the not very difficult conversion of an atheist; and we have naturalism too, for at the very beginning of the book the hero is a representative of flaming youth who rejects sage advice. In the *Arcadia*, Sidney stated the case for the twin deities Chance and Nature in order to reply with a passionate argument for divine Providence and Christian ethics. To ethical naturalism Spenser opposed Christian holiness and classical temperance, and against the metaphysical doctrine of flux he set up a medieval and Christian

compromise.   But in this period defences of
orthodoxy in morals, religion, politics, and economics, are too numerous to be catalogued.

On the relative weakness of anti-religious and
anti-ethical opinion in England a few general
observations may be made. One external cause was
strict censorship, and the cause of censorship
itself was the fear that any kind of unorthodoxy
was a step toward sedition and anarchy, a fear not
unjustified in a small country struggling to maintain itself against the great Catholic powers and
against internal conspiracies supported by those
powers.   Even if men had achieved our self-
conscious ideals of individual freedom, they would
have said that no sacrifice was too great for the
preservation of order. Then by nature as well as
by circumstance English humanists, both Catholic
and Protestant, were more completely and firmly
entrenched behind the ramparts of church and
state than their continental brethren. Nature and
circumstance also combined to make the English
humanists relatively less concerned with abstract
speculation and much more with practical problems. Such general attitudes may, if one likes,
be set down as obscurantism and unphilosophic
naïveté, but one may prefer less disparaging terms.
If Englishmen are unanimous in their defence of
established authority, their principles are essentially those of the great body of continental human-

ists. But this solid, all-embracing orthodoxy is a dyke which the smallest stream of water may undermine, and every hole must be stopped. How complex, and how simple, the humanistic creed was we can see, for instance, in these words of Ascham's:

For he that can neither like Aristotle in logic and philosophy, nor Tully in rhetoric and eloquence, will from these steps, likely enough, presume by like pride, to mount higher, to the misliking of greater matters; that is, either in religion to have a dissentious head, or in the commonwealth to have a factious heart: as I knew one, a student in Cambridge, who for a singularity began first to dissent in the schools from Aristotle, and soon after became a perverse Arian against Christ and all true religion; and studied diligently Origen, Basilius, and St. Hierom, only to glean out of their works the pernicious heresies of Celsus, Eunomius, and Helvidius, whereby the church of Christ was so poisoned withal.

Thus the beginning of individual and national destruction is the first doubt of Aristotle or Cicero. If the chain of argument seems quaint, though Ascham was no fool, it becomes more philosophic in Hooker's great exposition of the beauty of tradition, order, and conformity. And in some respects Hooker is a more typical Christian humanist than the rebellious individualist, Milton.

Scepticism and naturalism were monsters which to be hated had only to be seen. Another enemy of Christian humanism, sometimes allied with these but even more insidious when not, was the new science. It was not new, indeed, except in the prodigious extension and significance of its discoveries, for in the Middle Ages there had been men who gave up final causes as unknowable and turned to external nature as the only field of rational inquiry. Such a programme was, of course, fundamentally opposed to the humanistic concern with God, man, and society, and we have noticed already the traditional humanistic plea that scientific studies, like professional studies, do not teach us how to live well. For our purpose here it is enough to recall briefly the philosophic repercussions of pure and of applied science.

In the domain of pure science by far the most important advance was in astronomy, for speculation and observation undermined ideas and beliefs which had been accepted as eternal verities. Astronomy crystallized the great question, "What do I know?" in a vast and terrifying form. What had been a relatively small world, created by a fatherly God for the benefit of man, who was lord of all the rest of creation, became an infinite universe of universes moved by natural laws, a mechanical system in which human dignity shrank to nothing and God the Father became a logical postulate of motion. Of course these discoveries were not made, nor their implications realized, all at once; in fact they were stubbornly resisted, for various

good or less good reasons, and the process of general
acceptance was extremely slow. Yet thoughtful
men early understood enough to be confused and
unsettled. One might quote familiar expressions
of perplexity from Donne, but instead I will take
a few sentences from his contemporary Drummond,
who often echoed him:

The element of fire is quite put out, the air is but water
rarefied, the earth is found to move, and is no more the
centre of the universe, is turned into a magnet; stars are
not fixed, but swim in the ethereal spaces, comets are
mounted above the planets. Some affirm there is another
world of men and sensitive creatures, with cities and
palaces, in the moon: the sun is lost, for it is but a light
made of the conjunction of many shining bodies together,
a cleft in the lower heavens, through which the rays of
the highest diffuse themselves; is observed to have spots.
Thus sciences, by the diverse motions of this globe of the
brain of man, are become opinions, nay, errors, and leave
the imagination in a thousand labyrinths. What is all we
know, compared with what we know not?

If such questions were disturbing to religious
faith, they also shook the absolute authority of the
classics and the traditional humanistic discipline.
Along with the general antagonism between science
and humanism we may notice one factor peculiar
to this period. For the Renaissance the classics
were the literature of knowledge as well as of
power, and the earlier humanists were in a real
sense the party of progress, since a first necessity

was that the modern world should catch up with the ancient. But by the seventeenth century, when new knowledge and new kinds of knowledge had developed, advocates of science could say that classical science was obsolete, that the humanists constituted a party of reaction, an impediment in the way of progress. Here we have only to recall Bacon's attack on Ciceronianism as one of the three vanities or distempers of learning. Yet when Bacon names Ascham and, in condemnation, echoes a phrase of his, he is not doing justice to the man or the creed; for, as we have abundantly seen, to Ascham and to most other humanists good Latin stood, not for words as opposed to matter, but for a whole orthodoxy, cultural, ethical, political, and religious.

A more equal, if threadbare, illustration of the antithesis between humanism and the gospel of scientific progress is found, of course, in Montaigne and Bacon. Montaigne was certainly a humanist, even if not a Christian one, and Bacon has been happily described as a man who regarded the Church of England as a branch of the Civil Service and the Archbishop of Canterbury as the British minister for divine affairs; yet neither was hostile to religion and the antithesis between them is complete enough with that factor left out. The sovereignty of man, says Bacon in one of his massive phrases, lieth hid in knowledge. Montaigne would agree, but his terms would have an entirely different meaning. Bacon means that through scientific knowledge man can conquer external nature for his own use and benefit. Montaigne would mean that through study of his own inner strength and weakness man can learn to conquer himself. Bacon does not ignore ethics, but even in his essays he is showing chiefly how one may get on in the world by learning how to control other men; the humanists are concerned with ethics for the sake of the good life, and the keystone of their creed is religion. Bacon repudiates the study of first causes and applies himself to the study of things. To material progress he sacrifices that scale of divine and humane values which the best minds of antiquity, the Middle Ages, and the Renaissance had striven to make prevail. Bacon not only brought philosophy down to earth, he confined it within the four walls of a laboratory in which Paul and Aquinas, Erasmus and Milton, Socrates and Montaigne, would have suffocated. Of course we must acknowledge that at the time there was need of Bacon, and the new prophet found willing disciples.

While astronomical revelations and theories helped to cast a pall of melancholy over the mind of the early seventeenth century, applied science offered a message of infinite optimism. If Bacon retained any element of Renaissance human-

ism it was his sublime faith in the potential greatness of man. But whereas in such Christian
humanists as Pico and Erasmus and Milton, or
even in Montaigne, a similar faith is kept in check
by a sense of man's weakness, there is no such
check in the supposedly more realistic and modern
creed of Bacon. The Moses of scientific progress
proclaimed a new set of commandments with a
majestic finality worthy of Sinai, and for three
centuries mankind has been marching triumphantly
forward on the Baconian road, unaware for the
most part that a wilderness lay ahead as well as
behind. The great Victorian social critics saw the
hollowness of faith in mechanical progress, but it
is only of late years that their scepticism can be
said to have become part of the general consciousness. It is clear that man has conquered nature,
and it is no less clear that he has not conquered
himself. The fundamental questions asked by
Plato and Cicero, Erasmus and Montaigne, have
been neglected by believers in machinery, and in
our time they have been largely handed over to
psychologists, sociologists, and exponents of progressive education. A Renaissance humanist would
say that we had got out of the frying-pan into
the fire.

I am aware that to the modern-minded this
whole account of Christian humanism, with its
frequent repetition of such uninspiring words as

"orthodoxy," may seem only too obviously medieval and tame, a homely loaf of brown bread
compared with the brandy of bold speculation and
rebellion. But to the zealous humanist apparent
platitudes could be living realities—there is, after
all, no unbridgeable gulf between the Polonian
faith and the Apollonian—and this simple creed,
directly or indirectly, provided much of the solid
ideological foundation for the golden age of our
literature, the late sixteenth and earlier seventeenth
centuries. One might point out the more or less
strongly Christian humanism of such men as
Sidney and Spenser, Daniel and Chapman, who
preach rational control of the sensual impulses, and
who in larger ways represent the tradition by
virtue of their concern with aristocratic culture,
with humane values and the good life, and their
upholding of the established order. And even the
more complex and impersonal Shakespeare is no
less attached than the most orthodox humanist to
constituted authority, is no less scornful of the
mob. I had thought of devoting my fourth hour
to the discussion of humanistic ideas and ideals in
various kinds of imaginative and reflective writing,
but I changed my mind. Yet the subject must
not be ignored entirely, even if little can be said
in these few minutes—and Milton is looming up
on the horizon. I want to mention two major
premises of the serious writers of this age, and

they may be distinguished as ethical and meta-physical, if the words are not too ambitious for a couple of foot-notes.

In his famous discourse on the dignity of man Pico della Mirandola had proclaimed the completeness of human freedom and self-direction, but, like other Christian humanists, he had been conscious of man's frailty as well as of his greatness. Pico imagines the Creator concluding an address to man with these words:

"Thou shalt have power to decline unto the lower or brute creatures. Thou shalt have power to be reborn unto the higher, or divine, according to the sentence of thy intellect."

Thus to Man, at his birth, the Father gave seeds of all variety and germs of every form of life.

It is that simultaneous double vision of man which gives the literature of the English Renaissance its ethical strength and centrality, its heights and depths of tragic emotion. It is, to be sure, the mark of the greatest writers of all ages, especially the ancients, but the Christian religion exalted man's sense of his divinity and deepened his sense of bestiality; the distance between the two extremes is greater than it is in the most religious and philosophic of the classical authors. We may think, for example, of the difference in the range of feeling, of nobility and degradation, between Virgil's Aeneas and Shakespeare's Antony; the difference between Dido and Cleopatra is another matter.

While Renaissance writers look out upon a world which offers the widest tragic contrasts, the most appalling horrors, they themselves commonly stand in the centre, not on or beyond the margins, of the normal and ethical. Excess is excess and sin is sin—not self-expression. But in some later ages, when religion has lost its hold, the beast has been forgotten, and we have the literature of sentimental optimism. We may remember that a romantic has been defined as a person who does not believe in the fall of man. And in other ages, such as our post-war period, the god has been forgotten, and we have the literature of sentimental pessimism. We may remember that realism has been defined as romanticism on all fours. But in the great literature of the Renaissance man is both a god and a beast, and the greatest writer of the age is close enough to the Christian and classical traditions to see always with both eyes:

What a piece of work is a man, how noble in reason, how infinite in faculties, in form and moving, how express and admirable in action, how like an angel in apprehension, how like a god: the beauty of the world; the paragon of animals; and yet to me, what is this quintessence of dust?

These familiar words will serve to recall the whole texture of Shakespeare's thought and feeling, and one might add that hardly less familiar sentence in which Sir Thomas Browne plays magnificent variations on the double theme:

But man is a noble animal, splendid in ashes, and pompous in the grave, solemnizing nativities and deaths with equal lustre, nor omitting ceremonies of bravery in the infamy of his nature.

The other concept of the Renaissance mind, the metaphysical, is the macrocosmic complement of the ethical. Not only the soul of individual man but the whole world is the battle-ground between God and Satan. *Macbeth* is not simply a drama of human ambition and human crime brought to an end by human resistance; hell and outraged heaven play a part. Macbeth and Lady Macbeth have leagued themselves with the powers of darkness and Malcolm and Macduff are the conscious instruments of the powers above. It might be said that such a concept springs from purely Christian tradition, yet the Greek dramatists even more than the Elizabethan link earth with heaven and hell. Orestes, like Hamlet, is not merely a son avenging his father's murder, he is an agent of Apollo in righting wrong (though Aeschylus goes on to invoke a higher ideal of justice).

The essential difference between the medieval and the modern mind, if I may violate my own initial warnings against such large terms, is that for the one the universe and human life constitute a divine order with a divine purpose, while for the other the universe and human life are either an ordered or a haphazard mechanism. And there is no doubt to which category the Renaissance mind belongs. Shakespeare does not simply reflect "the mixed and muddled scepticism of the Renaissance." ✓His sense of man's life as part of a supernatural world grows directly out of the medieval religious tradition, which was strong enough to absorb even the heroic pagan tradition. Shakespeare may have been sufficiently withdrawn from religion to see the natural man acting in a natural world, yet he is not so far withdrawn, in time or in temperament, that medieval religious concepts have lost their imaginative and emotional power over him. While most of his contemporaries are more obviously and firmly Christian, and he has often been regarded as a great heathen, even his imaginative world is conditioned by the religious and ethical values of Christian humanism.

It is the loss of that religious view of life which makes the modern literature of social forces and other merely mundane and human motives seem, in comparison, such a small pinched thing. No proletarian background, no dark inner world of the unconscious, can take the place of a stage which includes God and Satan, heaven and hell. Authors of the immediate present talk a good deal about a faith in Life as the sole and all-sufficient creed for the artist. He is to take a brave stand on

The fact of life with dependence placed
On the human heart's resource alone,
In brotherhood bonded close and graced
With loving-kindness fully blown,
And visioned help unsought, unknown.

Such an attitude is doubtless better than the defeatism which preceded it, yet the instinctive craving for something more appears in the effort of many recent writers to make a religion out of Marxism. Of course we cannot even if we would bring back a general belief in a supernatural world —though it is odd that our scorn for theology is equalled only by our eager acceptance of the infallible and successively self-contradictory dogmas proclaimed by science, psychology, and economics—but at any rate a glance over the last three centuries inspires doubts of the future adequacy of humanistic optimism cut loose from a sobering faith in something like original sin. Indeed it would be hard to name a modern expression of this optimistic faith in Life which could be put beside two poems that owe their fundamental power to a medieval belief in sin and a medieval *contemptus mundi*, that is, *The Waste Land* and *Ash Wednesday*.

IV Milton

As I HAVE SAID, I had thought of giving this fourth hour to the general expression of Christian humanism in the imaginative and reflective literature of the English Renaissance, but I changed my mind. Perhaps a wiser change of mind would have been to cut off the fourth hour, since a classic definition of a fugue might be applied to a series of lectures—a composition in the course of which themes come in one by one and people go out two by two. But, as I at least have found already, there is some relief in turning from spacious generalities to particular humanists, and a survey of English humanism which omitted Milton would be like St. Paul's without its dome. For Milton is the last great exponent of Christian humanism in its historical continuity. He contains in himself, with the modifications set by his age and his temperament, more than the normal virtues, and some of the normal defects, of the tradition.

It may be more candid than diplomatic to acknowledge at the start that admirers of Milton have always been, consciously or not, on the defensive. They certainly must be nowadays, when for the first time since the seventeenth century Milton has ceased to be an active force in poetry. We may think that modern poets could still learn something from him, and if the poets thought so too we might be spared some headaches. But, so far from being an influence in contemporary work, Milton is damned as the man who crushed the fruitful metaphysical movement and kept poetry in bondage for three centuries. Mr. Eliot has even complained of Milton's obscurity. One may have, as I have, a great admiration for Mr. Eliot's writing in both verse and prose and still find a certain pleasure in visualizing the author of *The Waste Land* as he struggles with the meaning of *Paradise Lost*.

Among the various reasons for Milton's unpopularity doubtless the chief one is that in his major poems he treated on a heroic scale, and with a too confident simplicity, themes and problems which seem remote and no longer of vital concern to us. We think in purely human terms and know that

> malt does more than Milton can
> To justify God's ways to man.

Instead of Milton, who expounds a lofty faith in God and human reason, we prefer a smaller poet like Donne, whose sceptical uncertainties and staccato realism are more congenial to a generation which has lost its way. Milton is too big, too sternly strenuous, to allow us to feel at ease in his presence; he could never be taken under the maternal wing of Christopher Morley. Like Dante,

Milton is not what P. G. Wodehouse would call a "matey" person. Put beside Chaucer or Shakespeare, with their crowd of human characters, with their benevolent interest, half humorous, half divine, in the stuff of common life, Milton seems cold, inhuman, an unapproachable Jehovah of poetry.

But this discourse is not supposed to be an arraignment of Milton. I am merely indicating a consciousness of these and all the other charges, old and new, and if some are damaging to Milton, some are damaging to the reader. My purpose is to outline the growth and the main principles of Milton's thought, with reference to our general theme. I say "main principles" because there are many subtleties and ramifications which must be neglected, at the risk of making his mind appear more simple than it was. I shall not, therefore, be discussing Milton's poetry as poetry, and in discussing his major ideas and attitudes I shall have to incur the guilt of repeating commonplaces both about him and about Christian humanism. There is no other way of showing that he is the last voice of an essentially medieval tradition, that, with due allowance for the lapse of five centuries, Milton stands shoulder to shoulder with that twelfth-century humanist—and defender of tyrannicide—John of Salisbury. Yet Milton appears at a moment when Christian humanism is succumbing to such internal and external enemies as have been described. In England and Europe generally, in the troubled period of Milton's lifetime, humanism has grown less religious and religion less humane. We shall try to see in him the normal fusion and the occasional friction of classical and Christian elements. We shall try to see also what a noble anachronism the old humanistic faith has become in an increasingly modern and scientific world.

Milton's ardent study began in childhood and, no less than Bacon, he took all knowledge for his province. It was partly as a young Baconian, partly as a young Platonist, that he attacked the sterile Aristotelianism of the Cambridge curriculum and pleaded for genuine and fruitful examination of man's outer and inner world. What might be called Milton's academic valedictory, on the theme that learning brings more blessings to men than ignorance, at first sight seems only a tissue of Renaissance platitudes. But it also sets forth an intensely personal faith, the boundless optimism and ambition of a young idealist of genius who feels himself standing on the threshold of a new era, who sees no obstacle in the way of man's conquest of nature and of all individual and social problems. And he aspires, with a half-concealed but proud self-confidence, to be one of the makers of that new era, to be the oracle of many nations, whose home comes to be visited as a shrine. When we follow the course of Milton's life and work, we can measure the depth of his later pessimism only by appreciating the sublime and, as we cynically say, the unrealistic optimism of his earlier years.

That is one aspect of Milton's youthful humanism. We have other aspects in his Latin poems. These too are outwardly conventional—as long as bishops and beadles were subject to mortality Milton did not lack a theme—but in the personal pieces the obscurity of a learned language encouraged the young poet to express his own moods with more spontaneous frankness than he allowed himself in his native tongue. It is springtime and Cupid is busy everywhere. The young man's pulses are stirred by the awakening life of nature and by the beauty of girls in the parks, yet they are no Corinnas or Circes, and Milton's sensuous paganism is quite innocent. Indeed, lest he give a wrong impression, he assures his friend Diodati that, like Ulysses, he clings to the magical herb moly, by which he means Christian virtue. Thus the young Renaissance artist and the young puritan live in happy harmony together and, while Milton is finding that he cannot subscribe slave by taking holy orders, he has conceived of heroic poetry as a not less but more sacred and exalted calling. No other English poet has so earnestly and so repeatedly dedicated himself to the classical office of poet-priest, and most of his important poems may be regarded, directly or indirectly, as successive spiritual stock-takings.

We may read *L'Allegro* and *Il Penseroso* simply as tone poems, two ideal moods of a bookish and high-minded young man in the country, as lovely expressions of a serene tranquillity which their militant author never again enjoyed. But these companion pieces, written probably during Milton's later days at Cambridge, we may take also as an *ave atque vale*, a half-unconscious good-bye to carefree youth and an embracing of a life of mature seriousness. Keats, surveying Milton's work as a whole, discerned in him a conflict between the pleasures and the ardours of song, a conflict which is writ large in Keats himself. In Milton's twin poems there is no conflict as yet, but we who know what is to come can foresee possible discord between two modes of art and life. In fact he had already, in his sixth elegy, contrasted the irresponsible singer of wine and gaiety with the ascetic poet of truly heroic themes. And in the sonnet on his twenty-fourth birthday, written, it would seem, after the two lyrical pieces, Milton pledges himself to a religious life:

> Yet, be it less or more, or soon or slow,
> It shall be still in strictest measure even
> To that same lot, however mean or high,
> Toward which Time leads me, and the will of Heaven.

> All is, if I have grace to use it so,
> As ever in my great Task-Master's eye.

In this solemn acceptance of the divine will we are accustomed to hear the puritan note, the sense of personal responsibility to God, but these lines are also a partial echo of one of the most religious of ancient poets, Pindar.

When we look forward five or six years to the most elaborate and impassioned of Milton's earlier self-examinations, namely *Lycidas*, we find that the cheerful and the thoughtful ideals are no longer complementary but antagonistic. "L'Allegro," we might say, raises his voice for the last time to ask:

> Alas! what boots it with uncessant care
> To tend the homely, slighted, shepherd's trade,
> And strictly meditate the thankless Muse?
> Were it not better done, as others use,
> To sport with Amaryllis in the shade,
> Or with the tangles of Neaera's hair?

But Milton has put away childish things, and "Il Penseroso" replies, in a sterner mood than his earlier self had felt:

> Fame is the spur that the clear spirit doth raise
> (That last infirmity of noble mind)
> To scorn delights and live laborious days. . . .

If the whole passage on the heavenly reward of the virtuous and arduous life, for all its classical ornament, suggests that Milton's Hebraic zeal is

drying up his aesthetic sensibility, we may remember the letter written to Diodati in the same
year as *Lycidas*. In it Milton declares his God-
given passion for beauty in all the forms and
appearances of things. The words are both an
aesthetic and a religious affirmation.

The conflict in Milton has more than one
aspect. He felt keenly both the charms of con-
templative retirement and the duties of the active
life. But that conflict did not become a reality
until he returned from abroad in 1639. A more
immediate problem for a young poet of the
Renaissance was the conflict between the sensuous
and the ethical impulses in his nature. There was
never, of course, any question of an actual lapse
from his own high standards of personal conduct,
but it was more difficult for him, with his temperament and in his age, than it had been for Spenser
to reconcile the two motives in his poetry. Three
years before *Lycidas* he had written *Comus*. The
traditional masque glorified youth and love and
jollity; *Comus* is a sermon on temperance. With
all the sensuous passions of a young man and a
poet, Milton still holds the precious moly and has
not stooped to sensual gratification. Comus is
allowed to plead the case for "natural" license,
but his arguments—like Satan's—betray their own
speciousness; he is the representative, not of true
freedom, but of slavery. And the Lady, meeting

him first on the level of the natural reason, rises
with "sacred vehemence" to the religious defence
of "sun-clad" Chastity. If her or Milton's ideal
seems at moments negative, there is a far more
powerful positive impulse which we can understand if we look back a little into his spiritual
evolution. In a pamphlet of 1642, defending
himself as usual, Milton recalled some of his
earlier reading. At first he had been captured
by the smooth elegiac poets of Rome, but their
fleshliness was less satisfying than their art.
He had passed on to the two famous renowners of
Beatrice and Laura. There grew the belief that
"he who would not be frustrate of his hope to write
well hereafter in laudable things, ought himself
to be a true poem; that is, a composition and
pattern of the best and honourablest things. . . ."
From Dante and Petrarch, Milton was led to the
fables and romances of knighthood, and such
works proved, not the fuel of loose living, but
incitements to virtue. Next came Plato, with
his lofty idealism, his conception of the Eros
which leads to divine knowledge and beauty.
And, finally, there was St. Paul, with his ultimate
claim that "the body is for the Lord, and the
Lord for the body." The ideal of chastity in
Comus, then, is not merely negative, it is a positive
and all-embracing way of life. And the best
evidence is found, not in the exposition of Pauline

or Platonic or Spenserian moral ideas, but in that
indefinable purity of tone which instantly possesses
and elevates us when we begin—

> Before the starry threshold of Jove's court
> My mansion is. . . .

Milton returned from his prolonged continental
travels to maintain himself as a private school-
master and to follow with eager interest the course
of events which was soon to issue in civil war.
But in such a time it was reserved only for God
and angels to be lookers-on, and Milton was not
God nor, except at rare moments, an angel. With
mingled zeal and reluctance he plunged into
pamphleteering. The heroic poem which was to
win immortal fame had to be indefinitely postponed
for the writing of prose tracts which are now,
except for scholars, mostly dead. But we need not
lament the twenty years Milton gave to prose and
public affairs. He would not have been Milton if
he had not been able to sacrifice his hopes to the
claims of public duty. He belongs to that great
tradition which stretches back through Spenser
and Dante to the writers of Greece and Rome, the
tradition of the poet who is an active citizen and a
leader of his age. To Milton the romantic notion
of the artist as an isolated or anti-social figure
would have been not only reprehensible but unintelligible. Further, though he knew the magni-
tude of his sacrifice, since poetry was his right

hand and prose his left, yet he had always desired the fame of a great leader, an oracle of nations, and his work as a publicist, if in one sense a forced betrayal of his destiny, was also an integral part of its fulfilment. It consoles him in his blindness to recall his defence of liberty, "Of which all Europe talks from side to side." Finally, the poetry itself was not altogether a loser. The noble sonnets on public men and events are close in spirit to the patriotic odes in which Horace reminded decadent Rome of the old Roman virtues. And the major poems were strengthened by their author's experience in the arena. As he says in one of his apologies for delaying his appointed task, the truly heroic poet must have, among other things, "insight into all seemly and generous arts and affairs." To echo Gibbon, the secretary to the Council was not useless to the historian of Pandemonium.

Most of us, if we have any radical instincts at all, manifest them in youth, and then our arteries harden and our heads soften. The circumstances of Milton's early life might well have made him a contented conservative, but the older he grew the more radical he became. I can barely mention the chief battle-fronts on which he served.

First in importance among his prose works stands *Areopagitica*, the most eloquent defence of individual liberty and the power of truth in the language. The tract is a vivid reminder of its author's double affiliations. In form it is a classical oration, but it grew out of a puritan controversy over the rights of religious minorities. While for the modern reader it stands alone, at the time it was unheeded by the host of other pamphleteers.

Milton's early notoriety was especially due to the treatises in which he pleaded for divorce on the ground of incompatibility. I will say just three things about these works. First, modern research has freed Milton from the odium of having begun the series during his honeymoon; we know now that he began it a year later. Secondly, his plea for easier divorce was based, not on a week-end view of marriage, but on a high conception of its sanctity, of that marriage of minds which the Bible and the law did not recognize. Thirdly, notwithstanding the common prejudice against Milton's "Turkish contempt of females," he did not ignore the right of women as well as men to release from unworthy mates. If Milton always regarded man as the superior being, so did everyone else; how many men really think otherwise now?

To proceed with the main ideas of the prose tracts, in religious faith Milton moved from trinitarianism toward Arian and other heresies— though in essentials the theology of *Paradise Lost* remained orthodox enough to darken Sunday afternoon for many generations of evangelical readers. Milton's huge treatise on Christian doctrine, which was not published till 1825, was an attempt to define his own beliefs and, apparently, to provide a fundamental creed which all Christians might accept. As for religion on its external or institutional side, he changed from Anglicanism to Presbyterianism; then, seeing that the Presbyterians did not want religious freedom but only wanted to be top dog, he became an Independent with a capital "I"; his final position was independency with a small "i." Milton himself declared: "I never knew that time in England, when men of truest religion were not counted sectaries"; and, as Sir Herbert Grierson says, "he *was* a sect."

In politics, the supporter of monarchy became the defender of the regicides, a champion of a free republic who observed Cromwell's growing power with uneasiness.

In education, Milton damned the logical studies of the universities as an asinine feast of sow-thistles and brambles, and urged a more practical and certainly a more heroically comprehensive curriculum. His letter on education is the last of the long series of humanistic treatises which had begun nearly three hundred years before, and it has all the main features of the tradition. It is aristocratic. It aims at training the ablest young men to be useful and cultivated citizens, not

8

scholars. In substance the programme is mainly
classical, though less predominantly literary than
that of most earlier humanists, for Milton recognizes the study of nature and science generally.
His emphasis on religion and virtue, on the discipline of the moral judgment and the will, is no
special mark of puritan zeal, for that had been
the chief end of Christian humanism in all ages
and all countries.

When we survey Milton's whole body of writing
in prose and verse, we see that his various ideas
and principles start from a passionate belief in the
freedom of the will. There, of course, he breaks
utterly with Calvinistic doctrine. Over a century
earlier Erasmus had challenged Luther on just that
ground. No humanist who had learned from the
ancients the dignity of human reason could accept
predestination and the depravity of man. In all
problems, divorce, religion, politics, education,
censorship of the press, Milton goes where reason
leads him. No ordinance, he declares—in words
which from a religious man at that time are rather
bold—no ordinance, human or from heaven, can
bind against the good of man. People have a way
of associating the classics with mellow Toryism,
but for Milton the classics were a trumpet and a
sword. While Milton the artist learned his art
chiefly from the ancient poets, to Milton the
humanist and publicist Athens and Rome were the

nurseries of individual and republican liberty. No wonder that Hobbes, recoiling from the chaos of the times to plead for absolutism in government, exclaims, with men like Milton in mind:

And by reading of these Greek and Latin authors men from their childhood have gotten a habit, under a false show of liberty, of favouring tumults, and of licentious controlling the actions of their sovereigns, and again of controlling those controllers; with the effusion of so much blood as I think I may truly say there was never anything so dearly bought as these western parts have bought the learning of the Greek and Latin tongues.

At the same time we should remember the Protestant conception of "Christian liberty" which Professor Woodhouse has emphasized, that aristocratic distinction between the regenerate and the unregenerate which in Milton coalesces with the aristocratic principle of classical humanism. And, to echo Professor Woodhouse further, Milton's classical humanism sets him apart from merely religious puritans and leads him to interpret the regenerate state in humanistic, that is, in rational and ethical terms.

Dr. Tillyard remarks that if Milton had been stranded in his own paradise, he would have eaten the apple and immediately justified the act in a polemical pamphlet. We need not query a cheerful epigram, but we may notice that romantic idea which is still to be met, outside universities— namely, that Milton was of the devil's party without knowing it, that Satan was his real hero. Certainly the Satan of the first two books of *Paradise Lost* would not be the splendid figure he is if Milton himself had not been a rebel against authority, yet we are intended to see that from the very beginning Satan's heroic strength is vitiated by a fatal taint. For Satan is an example, on the grand scale, of perverted reason and perverted will, and the later books record his progressively shameful degradation. Milton never fought for the right of the individual to do as he pleases. While the traditional orthodoxy of the humanistic creed was modified by Milton's vigorous individualism, none the less he conceives of liberty as the right of man's disciplined reason to self-government, and one who loves liberty must first be wise and good. Hence the supreme importance of education, above all in the sacred and humane writings which provide ethical as well as intellectual training.

It is no accident that Milton's four long poems deal with one great theme, the human will confronted by temptation. Among the various motives inherent in, or read into, the chosen fables, perhaps the most obvious and recurrent are the sensual. Such emphasis is partly puritan and partly Miltonic. Milton's first marriage, apparently, gave a shock to his self-confidence which reverberates in the poems composed many years

later. If he, a man elect, had not allowed his
senses to betray his reason, he had at least shown
a terrible lack of discernment. However large or
small the personal factor, and in our days it is
only too likely to be exaggerated, it is clear in the
first place that Milton's ethical doctrine was not
a copy-book abstraction but a vital reality which
was proved on his pulses. In the second place,
and this is what concerns us here, Milton's various
treatments of the theme of temptation are as
much classical as Christian. The battle is not
merely between the love of God and the sinful
flesh, it is between reason and unreason, "knowledge" and "ignorance." Milton uses the ethical
psychology of Plato which had contributed so
much to the rational framework of Spenser's moral
allegory. Plato's thought, as Professor Hughes
says, is built into the ethics of Milton's poems as
substantially as some parts of the Bible are built
into their plots. (One may sometimes wish for
more gleams in Milton of that white light of
Platonism which glows in Vaughan or Browne, but
in the main the humanistic tradition had been
unmystical.) If one may venture, in these days
of psychological laboratories when moral responsibility has been shifted to defective glands, to
recall again the naïve ideas of ancient thinkers, the
kernel of the matter is that reason, the highest

and most human of human faculties, should control
the irrational passions and appetites.

Here I must quote those eloquent and familiar
sentences from the central passage of *Areopagitica*
which explain the ethical substance and purpose
of Milton's major poems, explain indeed the whole
character of his Christian humanism. It may be
observed that his conception of God's plan that
human virtue should prove itself by resisting evil
is a favourite idea of Lactantius, and Milton
quotes him in his *Commonplace Book:*

I cannot praise a fugitive and cloistered virtue, un-
exercised and unbreathed, that never sallies out and sees
her adversary, but slinks out of the race, where that
immortal garland is to be run for, not without dust and
heat. Assuredly we bring not innocence into the world,
we bring impurity much rather; that which purifies us is
trial, and trial is by what is contrary. That virtue therefore
which is but a youngling in the contemplation of evil, and
knows not the utmost that vice promises to her followers,
and rejects it, is but a blank virtue, not a pure; her whiteness is but an excremental whiteness. Which was the
reason why our sage and serious poet Spenser, whom I dare
be known to think a better teacher than Scotus or Aquinas,
describing true temperance under the person of Guyon,
brings him in with his palmer through the cave of Mammon,
and the bower of earthly bliss, that he might see and know,
and yet abstain. . . .

Many there be that complain of divine Providence for
suffering Adam to transgress; foolish tongues! When God
gave him reason, he gave him freedom to choose, for reason

is but choosing; he had been else a mere artificial Adam,
such an Adam as he is in the motions. We ourselves esteem
not of that obedience, or love, or gift, which is of force:
God therefore left him free, set before him a provoking
object, ever almost in his eyes; herein consisted his merit,
herein the right of his reward, the praise of his abstinence.
Wherefore did he create passions within us, pleasures
round about us, but that these rightly tempered are the
very ingredients of virtue? . . .

This justifies the high providence of God, who, though
he commands us temperance, justice, continence, yet
pours out before us even to a profuseness all desirable
things, and gives us minds that can wander beyond all
limit and satiety.

This last sentence, with its verbal anticipations
of *Paradise Lost,* is a particular reminder of
Milton's method of justifying the ways of God to
men. He distorts the biblical fable in order to put
it on a humanistic and rational basis. Adam and
Eve do not simply disobey an arbitrary decree,
they allow their reason, their faculty of moral
choice, to be overruled by their passions and
appetites. Coming to *Paradise Regained,* the un-
instructed reader might naturally expect the subject to be the crucifixion and redemption, but the
doctrine of vicarious atonement, though central in
traditional Christianity, is distasteful to Milton;
he accepts it, of course, but in a dryly legal way.
For him paradise is regained when Christ, the
personification of ideal human reason and will,
conquers the conqueror of Adam.

But if Milton's ethical scheme is always rational, it is not always equally human and humane. In *Comus*, beautiful as the writing is, the ethical sermon, despite its Platonic and Christian radiance, has the unrealistic, inflexible assurance that goes with the exalted idealism of youth. In *Paradise Regained*, as Professor Rice has made clear, Milton is consciously trying to show Christ's human humility and constancy of faith; yet his hero is perfect and cannot sin, and the poem, as the presentation of a moral struggle and victory, is relatively unreal and cold. In *Paradise Lost*, Adam and Eve are at first artificial beings in an artificial world, but they are humanized by sin and suffering, and their author is too when he contemplates them. In dealing with the fall itself Milton turns from epic narrative to intimate drama, and the deep sympathy manifested there culminates in the marvellous close. The great cosmic and supernatural background, the epic war between God and Satan, which had been rendered with such heroic pomp and circumstance, with such sweep of imagination—all this, in Professor Stoll's words, gives place to a twilight picture of two human beings alone in the world:

> Some natural tears they dropped, but wiped them soon;
> The world was all before them, where to choose
> Their place of rest, and Providence their guide:
> They hand in hand, with wandering steps and slow,
> Through Eden took their solitary way.

Milton is an unfailing master of the classical quiet ending, but here, as in Greek drama, quietness means serenity only to those who miss the mingled tragedy and hope, irony and pity, in a symbolic picture of life itself reduced to its elemental terms. And if in *Paradise Lost* the theological frame melts away, no such frame obtrudes at all in *Samson Agonistes*. This, the one great English drama on the Greek model, is the most deeply humanized treatment of Milton's perennial theme, and it remains, not the most beautiful, but the most wholly alive, the most permanently moving, of all his works. Samson is a completely human being in a completely real world, a great man who has lived greatly and sinned greatly. If he differs from his Greek counterparts, Heracles, Prometheus, and the aged Oedipus, through his faith in the God of Israel, what we feel most is the tragic drama that goes on in Samson's own soul.

There is profound pessimism in the later books of *Paradise Lost*, and it reaches its depth in *Samson*, where the hero's triumphant martyrdom scarcely mitigates the effect of Milton's arraignment of God. The sheltered idealist had grown up thinking that England was full of John Miltons who had only to be shown the right way to follow it. In *Areopagitica* his optimism runs high. When God is beginning a new and greater reformation, "what does He then but reveal Himself to His servants, and, as His manner is, first to His Englishmen?" Among the first to be informed of divine intentions would be John Milton, who craved an honourable share in the great work. Now the fields are white for harvest; there can be no lack of reapers.

Methinks I see in my mind a noble and puissant nation rousing herself like a strong man after sleep, and shaking her invincible locks. Methinks I see her as an eagle mewing her mighty youth, and kindling her undazzled eyes at the full mid-day beam, purging and unscaling her long-abused sight at the fountain itself of heavenly radiance. . . .

Sixteen years later, when the wheels are moving rapidly to bring back Charles Stuart, Milton makes a last appeal for a free republic. But with all its detailed plans this tract is an admission of defeat. The vision of a noble and puissant nation has faded into the light of common day, and men worthy to be for ever slaves are rushing to put their heads under the yoke. The good old cause is dead, and the work of a large part of Milton's life is undone. While he seems, outwardly, to have had a fairly cheerful old age, the stress and stimulus of composition heightened his realization of heroic past and ignoble present. He can declare himself still able to sing with voice unchanged,

> though fallen on evil days,
> On evil days though fallen, and evil tongues,
> In darkness, and with dangers compassed round,
> And solitude,

but his voice is changed, even in these very lines.

Milton had never been a democrat in the modern sense of the word. He did not believe that one man's opinion was as good as another's. But, both as humanist and as puritan, he had believed passionately in the collective wisdom, inspiration, and effectual power of the best men, whether Platonic philosopher-kings or puritan "Saints." There is little of that faith left in his later works. Samson, God's chosen hero, is now "Eyeless in Gaza at the mill with slaves." Milton tries to find a basis for hope in the scroll of future history revealed to Adam, but Adam hears no such story of national courage and triumph as Aeneas heard from Anchises:

> Truth shall retire
> Bestuck with slanderous darts, and works of Faith
> Rarely be found; so shall the world go on,
> To good malignant, to bad men benign,
> Under her own weight groaning, till the day
> Appear of respiration to the just,
> And vengeance to the wicked. . . .

Milton's hope of a new reformation, then, will be realized only at the day of judgment, when the evil world is cleansed by fire, and that is small comfort here and now. But if his old faith in men has proved vain, something can still be done by individual man; he can at least rule himself. So when Adam has learned the rational and Christian

virtues, he has no need of an earthly paradise, he
has a paradise within him, happier far. So Christ,
man's perfect model, maintains his integrity
against the allurements of the world. So Samson,
resisting selfish and sensual temptations, achieves
an inner regeneration which makes his outward
fate of no account.

There are two special topics, both related to
Milton's Christian humanism, with which we may
end. When we think of his lifelong devotion to
the classical authors who taught him his craft,
who inspired alike his love of liberty and his love
of discipline, it cannot be other than a painful
shock to come upon that violent denunciation of
Greek culture in *Paradise Regained*. And the
shock is all the greater for the eulogy of Hellenism
which precedes it:

> Athens, the eye of Greece, mother of arts
> And eloquence, native to famous wits
> Or hospitable, in her sweet recess,
> City or suburban, studious walks and shades.
> See there the olive-grove of Academe,
> Plato's retirement, where the Attic bird
> Trills her thick-warbled notes the summer long....

And so on. But this beautiful evocation of Athens
and her legacy to the world, written from the heart
if ever anything was, is put in the mouth of Satan,
and in an almost strident voice Christ answers
with a repudiation of the vain philosophy, oratory,

and poetry of Greece, which cannot approach the sacred truth of Hebrew writings.

It is painful indeed to watch Milton turn and rend some main roots of his being, but we must try to understand him. His harsh condemnation is relative rather than absolute; we know that his favourite authors up to the end were ancients, and this very poem owes much to them. Yet, with a strenuous and disappointed life behind him, Milton has come more and more to hold fast to ultimate things. If he, a warfaring Christian, must choose between the classical light of nature and the Hebrew light of revelation, he cannot hesitate, whatever the cost. For if our supreme task in this world is the conduct of our own lives, then Christ comes before Plato. It would be wrong to say simply that in old age the puritan has conquered the humanist. What is true is that Milton holds the traditional attitude of the Christian humanist with a more than traditional fervour inspired by the conditions of his age and by his own intense character.

The place of the Bible and the church in the humanistic tradition we have seen, and Milton himself had always put the sacred writings first, even if his own reason had sometimes strained their elasticity. So this outburst in *Paradise Regained*, uniquely elaborate and vehement though it is, contains nothing essentially new. One could

trace a consistent attitude from the beginning.
We have seen how his conception of love and
chastity rose from Ovid to Plato and finally St.
Paul. Though the classics form the staple of his
educational programme, Milton expressly puts the
Bible on a higher level. In apologizing, as a
pamphleteer, for the postponement of that heroic
poem he is going to write, he affirms its superiority
to the ancient epics, not because he is a greater
artist than Homer and Virgil—as artist Milton is
humble enough—but because he is a Christian.
His epic is not "to be obtained by the invocation
of dame memory and her siren daughters; but by
devout prayer to that eternal Spirit, who can
enrich with all utterance and knowledge, and sends
out his seraphim, with the hallowed fire of his altar,
to touch and purify the lips of whom he pleases."
The claim is repeated in those several invocations
in *Paradise Lost* which, outwardly imitations of
classical addresses to the Muse, are really prayers.
And while throughout the poem he employs mytho-
logical allusions, many of them among the most
beautiful things he ever wrote, so sternly does he
feel that the highest truth must be kept pure that
again and again he takes pains to label these
myths pagan fiction. Such facts testify to the sin-
cerity and consistency of Milton's Christian faith.
They testify also to the dilemma facing a puritan
bred in the tradition of Renaissance classicism.

The second and last topic involves a similar question of apparent inconsistency. Along with temperance in the moral sphere Adam learns the necessity of temperance in the pursuit of secular and scientific knowledge. This is not an incidental but an integral part of Milton's subject, and we may ask how such a position can be taken by the man who had been receptive to Baconian ideas, who had given science an exceptional place in his educational scheme, and who had written with such power in defence of free inquiry. A partial answer to this question has, I hope, already been given. We have seen that from the Middle Ages onward the Christian humanists, under the banner of Cicero, Plato, and Christ, attacked the various tribes of Aristotelians because neither logic nor natural science, however good in themselves, taught the right conduct of life. For that highest wisdom, they said, one must go first to the sacred, secondly to the classical, authors. Like all intelligent men Milton was interested in the new astronomy, but, like all Christian humanists, he feared the danger of confusing wisdom and knowledge, law for man and law for thing. In 1642, for instance, he had distinguished between "that knowledge that rests in the contemplation of natural causes and dimensions, which must needs be a lower wisdom, as the object is low," and "the only high valuable wisdom," which is the knowledge of God and the true end of man's life.

In the following decades it might well seem that the rising tide of science and scientific philosophy threatened to sweep away religious and humane values altogether, and a consciousness of that movement, along with larger and sadder experience of life, would only intensify Milton's religious and humanistic reaction. Even if individual scientists retained their Christian faith, the implications of science seemed plain. For Milton as for Christian humanists of all ages (including the Cambridge Platonists), the physical and metaphysical world is a divine order with a divine purpose, and man is a being endowed with divine reason and divine will. For the scientific philosopher, such as Hobbes, the universe is a purely mechanical system of bodies moving in time and space. God and man alike have been pushed out of the real world, for real knowledge is mathematical knowledge. God is the initial cause of motion. The human faculties, which for the humanist are all that matters, have become mere bundles of secondary qualities which cannot be measured. The human mind is a blank wall which receives physical sensations. Memory, the mother of the Muses, is decayed sensation. The will, for Milton the helm of man's ship, is only the last, the effectual, appetite. Is it any wonder the

Christian humanist believes that free speculation
has undermined fundamental values, that Adam
is taught to check the roving mind or fancy, which
lures men into philosophic mazes, and to recognize
that the prime wisdom is that which illuminates
the moral problems of daily life?

The inevitable and basic antithesis which Miss
Nicolson has pointed out between Milton and
Hobbes is the same as that between Petrarch and
the Averroists—or between Arnold and Huxley.
The end of all learning and eloquence, said Erasmus, is to know Christ and honour Him. Of the
two definitions of education in Milton's prose
tract the less familiar but not less Miltonic one is
this:

The end, then, of learning is to repair the ruins of our first
parents by regaining to know God aright, and out of that
knowledge to love Him, to imitate Him, to be like Him,
as we may the nearest, by possessing our souls of true
virtue, which, being united to the heavenly grace of faith,
makes up the highest perfection.

Nearly a quarter of a century later that definition
is expanded, one might say, in Milton's final
summing-up of the lesson of *Paradise Lost*. If in
his early days he had had some Baconian dreams
of the conquest of nature, now, in his age, he has
no thought of an earthly paradise; Adam—to
repeat that all-important line—has a paradise
within him, happier far.

Obviously I am not trying to claim for Milton the dubious title of modernity. Throughout its long history Christian humanism had ranged itself in opposition to most of the tendencies which we choose to call modern; its values remained classical and medieval. They remained so in Milton. For all his rationality and radicalism, in his conceptions of God and man Milton stands with Erasmus and Petrarch and John of Salisbury and a host of others. All these evidences of medieval obscurantism in Milton and the humanistic tradition are such as make the modern liberal either shudder or smile. Christian humanism may be dismissed as an artificial and unrealistic reconciliation of essentially antagonistic elements, a spurious harmony doomed to early disruption. Yet it did mould the culture of centuries, and in the face of the secular and scientific movement it displayed remarkable strength. Some might say that Christian humanism could or should have prolonged its life by embracing science, by adapting itself to the march of mind. It might have done so, at the cost of losing its identity. Perhaps in the end it did do so. In modern times we have had many kinds of "humanism," good and less good, but they are not that of the Middle Ages and the Renaissance, and both literature and education—to go no further afield—have suffered accordingly.

We are all agreed, I suppose, that education
nowadays is in a state of chaos. We do not know
what we are doing, or why we are doing it. The
humanists did know. In saying that one expects,
of course, to hear at once that invaluable *cliché:*
"But we live in a vastly more complex world." The
humanists might have looked at their very complex
world and decided that the educational programme
needed to face realities, that it needed courses on
alchemy, astrology, the management of ordinaries,
the psychology of success at court, and various
other fine and useful arts of which the analogues
flourish in our curricula. The humanists, with their
limited vision, believed in selecting the best for
the training of the best.

Further, we have seen that the purpose of
English humanism in its great age was the pro-
duction of citizens, not scholars. (That did not,
by the way, mean the study of a gaseous thing
called civics.) The chief Renaissance humanists,
in common with most of the ancients, held a
didactic and religious view of literature. When
the vital flame of humanism died, when the study
of literature and rhetoric was divorced from the
study of virtue, science regained the ascendancy
it had held in the thirteenth and fourteenth
centuries. To hungry sheep who felt that they
were being fed on husks, the scientists seemed to
offer something real. If Renaissance humanism

succumbed to internal decay as well as to stronger
rivals, there is a moral perhaps for us official
custodians of the humanities. The modern world,
apart from proletarian authors, has long abandoned
the didactic and religious view of literature, and
the result has been irresponsible journalism on the
one hand and irresponsible scholarship on the other.
When literature ceases to be studied as a guide to
life, the zest for discovery begins. We might say
that the appearance of Bentley marked the death
of Renaissance humanism in England. In recent
times we have witnessed the virtual extinction of
the classics, and at present even the modern
humanities are yielding ground daily to the social
sciences. With much help from external enemies
we English scholars are toiling mightily to bring
about the death of English; it is a quaint thought
that if many of us had lived during the Renaissance
we would have been unregenerate Scotists, wrapped
up in our quiddities. We may survive for a time
as a somewhat vermiform appendix to economics
and sociology, and we may be of use in translating
the writings of professors of education into English,
but one may wonder, timidly, if a real revival of
the humanities might not be inaugurated by a
moratorium on productive scholarship—not too
long a moratorium, since good teaching and writing
do not grow out of soil that is never stirred up, but
long enough to restore our perspective and sense

of values. What a golden interlude we might have, with the learned journals temporarily withdrawn, with no scholarly lucubrations to read or write, no annual bibliographies to torment us with hundreds of things we must know if we are to be qualified to lead hopeful young men into the same labyrinth, with nothing to do, in short, but sit down in peace with the great books we ought to be soaking in! I did not intend to turn evangelist, and I must say that this mood, which may seem pathological, is really much more confessional than hortatory. But since I have gone so far in what may be called "sharing," I may mention a minute personal circumstance which is determined by the exigencies of wall space in my small study, but might also be taken as a spiritual allegory. In front of my desk are serried rows of card-indexes, bibliographies, and periodicals. Out of sight behind me are Holbein's portraits of Erasmus and More. "Saint Socrates, pray for us."

But I should like to end on a more inspiring and eloquent note, and that necessitates quotation from someone else. I do not know any briefer or better eulogy of the humanistic tradition than these words of Mr. Santayana's:

The oldest forms of life, barring accidents, have the longest future. New ideas in their violence and new needs in their urgency pass like a storm; and then the old earth, scarred and enriched by those trials, finds itself still under the same sky, unscarred and pure as before. The Latin language and the study of classic antiquity are the chief bond for western nations with the humanities, with the normalities of human nature; and this not merely by transporting us, as in a vision, to some detached civilization—as Greek studies might do if taken alone—but by bringing us down step by step through all the vicissitudes of Christendom to our own age, and giving us a sound sense for the moral forces and moral issues that now concern us. The merely modern man never knows what he is about. A Latin education, far from alienating us from our own world, teaches us to discern the amiable traits in it, and the genuine achievements; helping us, amid so many distracting problems, to preserve a certain balance and dignity of mind, together with a sane confidence in the future.

Index

Aeschylus, 98
Alexander, W. J., 13
Allen, J. W., 36
Ambrose, Saint, 44
Aquinas, Saint Thomas, 30, 35, 53, 85, 93, 118
Aretino, Pietro, 34
Ariosto, Lodovico, 38
Aristophanes, 43, 46
Aristotle, 30, 38, 46-8, 50, 52-4, 56, 73, 76, 79, 86, 89, 104, 127
Arnold, Matthew, 49, 129
Ascham, Roger, 75-9, 87, 89, 92
Augustine, Saint, 36, 44, 50, 52, 55, 59-60, 72
Averroes, 53, 55-6, 129

Bacon, Francis, 18, 33, 45, 60, 69, 92-4, 104, 127, 129
Baron, Hans, 58
Basil, Saint, 89
Bayle, Pierre, 14
Becket, Thomas, 47
Becon, Thomas, 77
Belloc, Hilaire, 28
Bentley, Richard, 73-4, 132
Boccaccio, Giovanni, 49
Bodin, Jean, 33
Browne, Sir Thomas, 98, 117
Bruni, Leonardo, 55, 58
Budé, Guillaume, 64, 78
Burckhardt, Jacob, 18-22, 24, 26-7, 31-2
Burdach, Konrad, 22-4

Calvin, John, 29, 83, 114
Castiglione, Baldassare, 58
Cecil, William, Lord Burghley, 79
Celsus, 89
Chambers, R. W., 73, 75, 78
Chapman, George, 95
Charlemagne, 25
Charles II, 122
Chaucer, Geoffrey, 29, 35, 49-50, 103

135

Cheke, Sir John, 74-6, 79, 87
Chesterton, G. K., 28
Chrysostom, Saint, 42
Cicero, 37, 42, 46, 48, 50-2, 54, 57-62, 65, 76-7, 83, 86, 89, 92, 94, 127
Colet, John, 64, 71-2, 75-6
Cromwell, Oliver, 113

Daniel, Samuel, 95
Dante, 23, 46, 57-8, 102, 109-10
Demosthenes, 76
Descartes, René, 33
Diodati, Charles, 105, 108
Dionysius the Areopagite, 71-2
Donne, John, 86, 91, 102
Drummond, William, 91
Duns Scotus, 118

Edward VI, 74
Eliot, T. S., 100, 102
Elizabeth, Queen, 74
Elyot, Sir Thomas, 72, 76, 78-9
Erasmus, Desiderius, 52, 60-8, 70, 72-3, 78, 82-3, 93-4, 114, 129-30, 133
Eunomius, 89
Euripides, 64

Feltre, Vittorino da, 34
Ficino, Marsilio, 56, 60, 71-2
Flora, Joachim of, 21
Francis of Assisi, Saint, 21-2
Fulgentius, 44

Gibbon, Edward, 15, 111
Green, J. R., 15
Grierson, Sir Herbert, 113
Grocyn, William, 71

Hallam, Henry, 15
Helvidius, 89
Henry VIII, 73, 75
Hesiod, 43
Hobbes, Thomas, 115, 128-9
Hody, Humphrey, 15

Holbein, Hans, 63, 133
Homer, 43, 126
Hooker, Richard, 34, 85, 89
Horace, 38, 46, 48, 111
Housman, A. E., 79
Hughes, Merritt Y., 117
Huxley, T. H., 129

Inge, W. R., 79
Isocrates, 76

Jerome, Saint, 52, 89
Juvenal, 48

Keats, John, 45, 106
Kingsley, Charles, 75

Lactantius, 52, 58, 118
Lanson, Gustave, 37
Latimer, William, 71
Lily, William, 71-2
Linacre, Thomas, 70-2
Livy, 36
Loyola, Ignatius of, 83
Lucian, 64, 86
Lucretius, 86
Luther, Martin, 36, 52, 65-7, 83, 114
Lyly, John, 87

Machiavelli, Niccolò, 36, 79, 87
Manutius, Aldus, 70
Marlowe, Christopher, 34, 86
Martial, 76
Mary, Queen, 74
Maurois, André, 27
Meung, Jean de, 29
Michelet, Jules, 18, 22, 27-8, 31
Milton, John, 14, 42, 69, 73, 78-9, 83, 89, 93-5, 101-30; *Areopagitica*, 111-12, 114, 118-19, 121-2, 127; *Comus*, 108-10, 120; Divorce pamphlets, 112, 114; *Il Penseroso*, 106-7; *L'Allegro*, 106-7; Latin poems, 105-6; *Lycidas*, 107-8; *Of Education*, 113-14, 126-7, 129;

Paradise Lost, 102, 112, 115-17, 119-24, 126-9; *Paradise Regained*, 119-20, 124-5; *Prolusion vii*, 104-5; *Samson Agonistes*, 121, 123-4
Mirandola, Pico della, 56, 60, 71-2, 94, 96
Modoin, Bishop, 25
Montaigne, Michel de, 36-7, 92-4
More, P. E., 17, 57
More, Sir Thomas, 71-3, 75, 78-9, 83, 87, 133
Morris, William, 28
Murray, Gilbert, 79

Newman, J. H., 75
Nicolson, Marjorie, 129
Nietzsche, Friedrich, 21
Nordström, Johan, 26

Origen, 89
Ovid, 45, 48, 76, 126

Pater, Walter, 22, 25
Paul, Saint, 57, 71, 83, 93, 109, 126
Petrarch, 23, 49-56, 60, 77, 82, 109, 129-30
Phillimore, J. S., 73, 78
Pindar, 107
Plato, 41-3, 46, 48, 50, 52, 54-7, 59-60, 62, 65, 71-3, 76, 83, 94, 104, 109-10, 117, 120, 123-8
Plautus, 76
Plotinus, 56, 72
Plutarch, 46
Poggio Bracciolini, 70
Pomponazzi, Pietro, 86
Prynne, William, 41

Quintilian, 46

Rabelais, François, 72
Ralegh, Sir Walter, 86
Ramus, Peter, 81
Rand, E. K., 66
Rastell, John, 87
Renan, Ernest, 51
Rice, Warner G., 120
Rienzo, Cola di, 23

Salisbury, John of, 47-9, 51-2, 60, 76, 82, 103, 130
Salutati, Coluccio, 55
Sandys, George, 45
Santayana, George, 133-4
Savonarola, Girolamo, 29, 71, 83
Scaliger, J. C., 78-9
Schirmer, W. F., 70
Seebohm, Frederic, 15
Seneca, 42, 48, 50
Shakespeare, William, 44, 95-9, 103
Sidney, Sir Philip, 78, 87, 95
Smith, Sir Thomas, 79
Socrates, 62, 93, 133
Spenser, Edmund, 38, 73, 78, 87, 95, 108, 110, 117-18
Spingarn, J. E., 45
Stoll, E. E., 120
Storrs, Sir Ronald, 79
Sturm, John, 60, 77
Symonds, John Addington, 28-9

Terence, 48, 76
Tertullian, 83
Tillyard, E. M. W., 115
Tiraboschi, Girolamo, 15
Toffanin, Giuseppe, 24, 53

Valla, Laurentius, 60-1, 64, 71
Varro, Marcus Terentius, 50
Vaughan, Henry, 117
Vicomercato, Francesco, 86
Virgil, 42, 44, 47, 50, 62, 96, 123, 126
Voigt, Georg, 19-20
Voltaire, 14

Wilson, Thomas, 79
Woodhouse, A. S. P., 115

Xenophon, 76

Zimmern, Sir Alfred, 79